100 YEARS OF
THERAF
1918 - 2018

For my father,

**Acting-Sergeant
Harold 'Alec' Lepine,**

Royal Air Force.

Mike Lepine

First Published Danann Publishing Ltd 2018

CAT NO: DAN0375

Photography courtesy of

Getty images:

Print Collector	Hulton Archive / Stringer
Popperfoto	Hulton Deutsch
Central Press / Stringer	Walter Nurnberg
Science & Society Picture Library	Charity / Stringer
Michael Dunning	United News/Popperfoto
Interim Archives	Andrew Yates / Stringer
Charles Hewitt / Stringer	

All other images, Wiki Commons

Book layout & design Darren Grice at Ctrl-d

Tom O'Neill Copy Editor

Made in EU.

ISBN: 978-1-912332-12-0

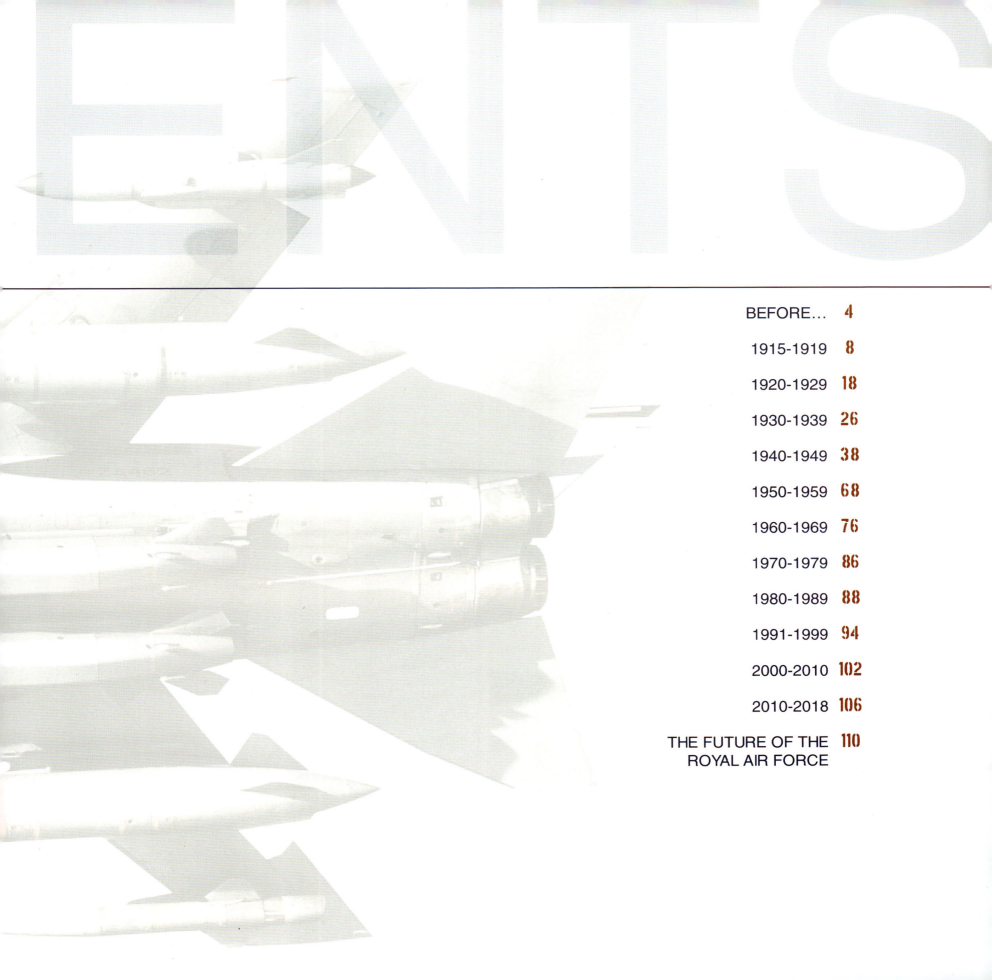

The first aeroplane flew in 1903. Barely eight years later, aeroplanes were being used for war. In 1911, an Italian airman named Giulio Gavotti flying a Etrich Taube monoplane dropped four hand grenades on an Ottoman military camp in Libya. He didn't hurt anyone, but that wasn't the point. That very same year, the Institute of International Law in Madrid tried unsuccessfully to get laws passed to prevent aeroplanes being used to bomb cities, limiting their role in war strictly to reconnaissance. It was far too little, and far too late. Some nations had long understood the potential of aeroplanes in future wars and an *'aviation arms race'* was already underway.

When Louis Bleriot flew the first Channel crossing in 1909, H.G. Wells said woefully of Britain, *'we have fallen behind in the quality of manhood.'* By the end of that year, the French Army could boast its very own air force comprising some 200 aeroplanes. The German Army had obtained its first machine the previous year and was busy assessing its potential as both the German Army and Navy simultaneously built up their fleets of giant Zeppelin airships. Even the Bulgarians were prepped for action. By contrast, in 1909 The War Office in Britain ended all work on military aircraft at Farnborough. It was judged too expensive.

It took Britain two years to get back in the race, when it was finally understood that aeroplanes could provide a more cost effective way to deliver reconnaissance and artillery spotting functions than those methods presently used. There was, it seems, a future for British military aviation after all. In 1911, the Balloon Section of the Royal Engineers officially became the Air Battalion. Pilots had to obtain their own Aviator's certification (although they would be refunded later) at a cost of £75. Other skills considered essential were the ability to sketch and to have the attributes of *'a good sailor'*.

When news of the aerial bombing in Libya finally got through, a sub-committee of the British Imperial Defence Staff was convened to look at the future of military flying in Britain. This committee recommended setting up a dedicated flying corps consisting of a military wing, a naval wing, a flying school, a reserve and an aircraft factory. On 13 April 1912, the Royal Flying Corps was established by Royal Warrant. The Air Battalion merged with the RFC a month later. By year's end, the RFC had twelve balloons and thirty six aeroplanes under its command, but it was chronically underfunded. Germany alone was spending over 700% more on its air power.

It was also clear from the very beginning that the army wing and the navy wing of the RFC would not sit easily together. Each had a separate commander within the RFC and each had very different visions and objectives. The Army wanted

the RFC for battlefield reconnaissance and artillery spotting. The Royal Navy wanted the capability to go after enemy submarines to prevent a naval blockade of Britain and also to bomb Zeppelin sheds, as airships posed a direct threat to Navy bases and dockyards. Neither liked a rival service having any say in what they did. By the start of 1914, the internal tensions within the RFC were just too strong: The Royal Navy broke away and formed the Royal Naval Air Service (RNAS) on 1 July 1914. The First World War began the following month.

The RFC, which was now exclusively an Army air force, found the aeroplane an essential tool almost straight away. Reconnaissance flights in the Mons area provided valuable information on German troop concentrations for the British Expeditionary Force, although this alone could not turn the tide of the German onslaught in those desperate first months.

Much has been made of the spirit of comradeship that existed amongst aviators from opposing sides during the early part of the war. Cheery waves and salutes were indeed exchanged — but it was always going to change, because enemy reconnaissance flights needed to be stopped. Salutary waves turned to shaking fists and bellowed insults. Rocks were thrown, along with nets, chains and rope in an attempt to snag the enemy's propeller. Aviators started packing pistols, then rifles and shotguns. The advent of

the machine gun was inevitable. Vickers had been experimenting with mounting machine guns on aircraft as long ago as 1912. It was, however, the developments of first the French and then the Dutch in 1915 in being able to shoot forward through a propeller that enabled the creation of the first true fighter aircraft.

The development of the bomber proved more problematic. Even when on the rare occasion a bomber could find its target — and then actually hit it — its payload was usually far too insignificant. On the actual battlefield, the bomber's power was as nothing compared with the devastation delivered by artillery barrages. Away from the battlefield, however, the bomber could have quite another effect…

BELOW 4 IMAGES L–R: Winston Churchill With Naval Wing of the Royal Flying Corps, 1914; The aeroplane sheds of the Royal Flying Corp at Farnborough, PRE-1914; A Sergeant of the Royal Flying Corps demonstrates a C type aerial reconnaissance camera fixed to the fuselage of a BE2c aircraft, 1916; Factory during First World War

HUGH TRENCHARD THE 1ST VISCOUNT TRENCHARD

Hugh Montague Trenchard was born the son of a Taunton solicitor in 1873. His military career took him first to India and then South Africa where, during the Boer War, he took a bullet in the chest that severely damaged one lung and left him partially paralysed below the waist and dependent on crutches. Advised by his doctors to vacation in Switzerland on health grounds, boredom quickly made him take up bobsleighing. A violent crash on the Cresta Run led to a miraculous outcome: Trenchard literally walked away, cured of his paralysis. A week later he won the 1901 St. Moritz Tobogganing Club's Freshman and Novices' Cups.

It was a friend who first suggested that Trenchard learn how to fly. Trenchard was intrigued and — despite that friend being killed in a plane crash only the previous day — he took instruction at Thomas Sopwith's Flying School at Brooklands. Trenchard was now 39 — one year off the maximum age for military pilots — and managed to get his certificate, despite his instructor revealing that the process had been 'no easy performance'. From here, he moved on to the military's Central Flying School, who did not initially know about Trenchard's poor flying skills as bad weather had shut down all flying. Trenchard now joined the staff and, since one of his tasks was to mark school papers, he set his own exam to gain his 'wings' and marked it himself. Naturally he passed. As the weather improved, his deficiencies became more obvious. No one took away his wings, but he was confined to teaching students strictly on the ground, and soon earned the nickname 'Boom' for his roaring but monotonous teaching voice.

When the Great War broke out, Trenchard was appointed as Officer Commanding the Military Wing of the Royal Flying Corps. A year later, he was made a brigadier-general and Officer Commanding the RFC in France. Trenchard would remain in the post until early 1918, pioneering ground support techniques and using the RFC in an aggressive, hard-hitting way. In December 1917, he was summoned to London and offered the position of Chief of the Air Staff (CAS) with the RFC and the forthcoming Royal Air Force. Sensing the difficult politics that came with the role, Trenchard was initially reluctant but pressured to accept. He resigned three months later, his resignation coming into effect just days after the RAF had been established.

Trenchard was offered a variety of new positions, all of which he turned down. It was only when he overheard himself being talked about as a 'traitor who should be shot' that he accepted the role of GOC of the 'Independent Air Force', a new bomber initiative designed to take the war to Germany. He served until the end of the war. It was Churchill who persuaded him to return to the RAF as Chief of the Air Staff in 1919.

Over the next ten years, Trenchard would establish the foundations and core values of the Royal Air Force as they are still recognised today. He would also become known as 'the father of the RAF' — a sobriquet he thoroughly hated.

MAIN IMAGE: Portrait of Hugh Trenchard

ABOVE: Major Hugh Trenchard at the Central Flying School, Upavon

TERROR FROM THE SKIES — THE FIRST BLITZ

Just before midnight on 31 May 1915, German Army Zeppelin LZ.38 flew over the North London suburb of Stoke Newington at a height of two miles. The first-ever air raid on London was underway. LZ.38 was around 530 feet long and carried with it 120 bombs, mostly incendiaries. It began dropping them, hitting a house in Alkham Road where the occupants were shaken but managed to escape. From Stoke Newington, the Zeppelin motored south, dropping more bombs on Hackney and Shoreditch.

At the time of the attack, London was defended by just 16 anti-aircraft guns. None of the guns spotted the Zeppelin. Fifteen RNAS fighters were launched to intercept LZ.38, but only one found the airship and suffered catastrophic engine failure before being able to engage. The pilot was killed on landing.

In reality, the attack left seven Londoners dead and a further 35 injured — but rumours swiftly swept the capital that hundreds if not thousands had been butchered, among them an entire theatre audience, and that much of London had been left in flames. Ferocious anti-German rioting broke out, denouncing the Zeppelin crews as *'baby killers'* and mobs looted shops with German-sounding names. It very quickly became all too clear to the authorities that the public outrage in response to any air raids would be out of all proportion to the actual casualties they caused. More Zeppelin attacks followed on both the capital and other English towns and cities. Public outrage — and fear — grew.

The government brought in new (and more) anti-aircraft guns and ten Home

LEFT: WW I poster, 1915

ABOVE RIGHT: Wrecked Zeppelin brought down near Essex, 1916

BELOW RIGHT: Bomb damage to property in Streatham, London caused by the German Zeppelin raid on the night of 23 - 24 September 1916

Defence squadrons were set up as the RFC assumed responsibility for Home Defence from the RNAS — but the public had already seen how ineffective these had been. When nine German Navy airships returned on the night of 31 January 1916, they completely missed Liverpool (their intended target), but instead dropped their payloads on the Black Country. 61 people died. 22 aircraft took off to intercept, but none found the airships and six of the planes crashed while attempting to land again.

'Hit back! Don't wait and see!' thundered the Daily Mail. The problem was, Britain had nothing to hit back with. It also had no proper aerial defence plan. Demands from the Army, heavily engaged on the Western Front, drained even the meagre resources that could otherwise be deployed to defend British cities.

UNDER PRESSURE

In February 1916, a government committee was set up under Lord Derby to look at the problem. Among its recommendations was that the RNAS and RFC should be amalgamated once more into one new dedicated air force — but this was thought impossible to achieve during wartime. In May, the newly constituted Air Board under Lord Curzon also recommended integrating the RNAS and RFC to form a separate air service controlled by a new 'Air Ministry'. Unwilling to lose control of their own aircraft, the Army and Navy vehemently opposed any such idea.

ZEPPELINS IN FLAMES

The Zeppelin raids continued and nothing much changed — until the night of 3 September 1916, when German Army SL.11 had the great misfortune to meet the BE2c piloted by Lt. William Leefe Robinson. Caught in multiple searchlights over Ponders End, the airship crew would have had little fear of the fighter. At worst, bullets from a Lewis gun could only rip tiny holes in

the gas bags that could be patched in flight. They had no idea that Leefe Robinson was carrying new experimental incendiary ammunition developed by a member of the famous Brocks Fireworks family. The rear of the Zeppelin ignited and flames began to spread. The airship was rocked by two explosions so huge that Londoners miles away were shaken from their beds and tumbled out into the streets to see what was happening. It's thought that half of London's population (including the author's aunt) witnessed the awe-inspiring sight of the gigantic airship burning high in the sky, before tipping up on one end and sinking to earth. No one on board survived.

Leefe Robinson's *'kill'* earned him a promotion and a Victoria Cross, and he became an instant celebrity complete with signed postcards to hand out to fans. Mired in the fight with the armed services over the possibility of any new independent air service, the government felt a sense of distinct relief. If British aircraft could find Zeppelins, they could now kill them. Airships however, were about to be replaced with a new, more powerful threat to the populace…

GOTHAS OVER LONDON

On the night of 26 May 1917, the Germans launched Operation Türkenkreuz (Turk's Cross). Twenty three giant Gotha bombers with 80 feet wingspans took off to bomb London. They couldn't find it - and instead bombed Folkestone where 95 people died. On 13 June, the Gothas finally found London. It was the first daylight bombing raid on the city and 162 died — including 18 children attending an infant's school. A further 432 civilians were injured. Ninety-two British interceptors went up to target the bomber fleet, but they could not climb fast enough to reach the Gothas before they headed away for home. On 7 July, the Gothas returned, killing a further 57 and bringing terror and chaos to the very heart of London by unloading three tons of bombs. A number of ministers and other senior figures, called that day to a meeting in Downing Street, witnessed for themselves the utter panic in the streets of Westminster amid the furious rattling of the air raid buzzers and the drone of the giant bombers overhead. *'One would have thought the whole world was coming to an end,'* said Sir William Robertson, the Chief of the Imperial General Staff, rather disapprovingly. Another equally unsympathetic witness described seeing *'a stampede of shrieking creatures'*.

Britain had seen off the Zeppelin scourge, only to suffer a new threat from

bomber aircraft. When the Gothas switched from day to night raids, they may have been less effective but the terror level felt by the British people only increased. Once again, demands were made on the government to do something. Britain had not been *'so humiliated since the Dutch Fleet sailed up the Thames in 1667,'* roared The Daily Mail and called for heads to roll both in the military and in government. Prime Minister David Lloyd George was besieged by demands in the Houses of Parliament that an entire German town should be obliterated each time a raid was launched on London. The RFC and the RNAS simply couldn't do it.

ABOVE: Bomb damage to property in Hither Green, London, following the German air raid on the night of 19 - 20 October 1917

LEFT: The damage done by a German Zeppelin bomb, World War I

NEW RECOMMENDATIONS

After the panic in Westminster caused by the Gotha raid of 7 July, Lloyd George took decisive action. Within just four days, General Jan Christian Smuts was instructed to examine the organisation of Britain's air resources and the conduct of aerial operations. In this, he proved to be something of a visionary. In his report, published in August 1917, he foresaw a future in which air power might dominate over all else:

'..the day may not be far off when aerial operations with their devastation of enemy lands and destruction of industrial and populous centres on a vast scale may become the principal operations of war…'

Just as in 1916, Smuts concluded that what was needed was an independent air force, formed by merging the RFC and the RNAS. He also concluded that a vital part of this new service would be a mighty bombing force capable of taking the war to Germany. Germany would either be crippled by the collapse of public morale, or at least dissuaded from the terror bombing of Britain.

What was needed, Smuts ultimately concluded, was an Air Ministry — and a Royal Air Force.

SETTING UP A ROYAL AIR FORCE

With the new threat of the Gotha raids, the government's need to be seen to be doing something now overrode the Army and Navy's objections. Plans proceeded with a speed only possible in wartime. On 29 November 1917, an Act of Parliament establishing the RAF received its Royal Assent.

LEFT: Officers of the newly formed Royal Air Force, some still wearing the uniform of the Royal Flying Corps, 1st April 1918

THE SOPWITH CAMEL

The Sopwith Camel first arrived on the Western Front in the summer of 1917, and, armed with twin synchronised .303 Vickers guns, is credited with shooting down 1,294 enemy aircraft. A difficult and even dangerous aircraft to fly, especially for inexperienced pilots, its flight characteristics nevertheless gave it the ability to out-manoeuvre and out-turn virtually anything else in the sky during a dogfight. With typical black humour, early pilots said that the Camel offered the choice between *'a wooden cross, the Red Cross and the Victoria Cross'*. Variants included a night fighter (the *'Comic'*), ground attack aircraft, two seater trainer and the 2F.1, which was designed to fly off early aircraft carriers.

Over 5,000 Camels were built, but by the time the RAF became active it was starting to be outperformed by new German warplanes like the Fokker D.VII. All Camels were retired from RAF service by the start of 1920, having been replaced by the Sopwith Snipe.

MAIN IMAGE: Royal Flying Corps with their Sopwith Camels and a rotary engine in northern France, circa 1917

OPP. PAGE TOP LEFT: Line diagram of Sopwith Camel

OPP. PAGE TOP: Sopwith Camels aboard the HMS Furious

OPP. PAGE MIDDLE: Sopwith Camels of No. 28 Squadron, Italian Front

OPP. PAGE BOTTOM: RFC Sopwith F.1 Camel in 1914-1916 period

THE RAF GOES TO WAR

Despite all apprehension, the new RAF settled into its role smoothly and efficiently on 1 April 1918. On the Western Front, the Germans were in the midst of a major offensive. Flying in support of the Army, the fledgling service helped to stop the German tide and then further assist as the Allies launched their own counter offensive, achieving almost complete dominance of the skies.

Giant Handley Page 'Bloody Paralyser' bombers had been taking the war to Germany since the winter of 1917. Within just a month of the RAF's formation, it had already established a prototype of 'Bomber Command' under the command of Hugh Trenchard, comprising nine squadrons of bombers and a further squadron of Sopwith Camel fighters for escort duties. Called 'The Independent Air Force', it operated without regard for the military needs of the Western Front and instead attacked the blast furnaces and poison gas manufacturing plants of Frankfurt, Cologne and Mannheim by night and by day. Between 6 June and 10 November 1918, the Independent Force launched 239 raids and dropped 550 tons of bombs. As in Britain, the raids had little military impact, but the effect on the morale of the German populace was huge and damning.

THE PRICE OF VICTORY

By the time the war ended on 11 November 1918, the Royal Air Force was already the strongest and largest air force in the world, with over 22,600 aircraft, 188 combat squadrons and almost 300,000 men under its command. It was also the world's first independent air force. In wartime it was superb. In peacetime it was an intolerable burden on the taxpayer.

With the Great War done, politicians eager for a peace dividend almost immediately began to question the need for the RAF. After all, they had just fought the *'war to end all wars'*. In August 1919, the government officially adopted *'The Ten Year Rule'*, a set of guidelines that assumed Britain would not be involved in any significant war within the next ten years. Military expenditure would be slashed in line with this assumption. Money was not the sole influencing factor. Given the unprecedented carnage of the First World War, with millions dead and many millions more maimed, society now looked upon anything militaristic with genuine revulsion. The very thought of another war was disgusting and few felt like building up armies, navies or air forces to contribute to tomorrow's slaughter.

This was recognised almost immediately. Winston Churchill, now Secretary of State for War and Air, fired Sir Frederick Sykes (who had followed Trenchard as CAS of the RAF) and instead brought Trenchard back once more. Trenchard could, Churchill was told, *'make do with little and would not have to be carried'*.

As the new RAF was assailed with demands for drastic cuts, Trenchard struggled to find a compromise and a meaningful new role for a peacetime RAF, saying of it:

'…the necessities of war created it in a night, but the economics of peace have to a large extent caused it to wither in a day, and we are now faced with the necessity of replacing it with a plant of deeper root …'

Trenchard saw the future of the RAF as primarily the continuance of the Independent Air Force — a strategic force of bombers providing both a deterrent and a means to strike at the enemy heartland:

'…in future the main portion of (the RAF) will consist of an Independent Force …. It may be that the Independent Air Force will grow larger and larger, and become more and more the predominating factor in all types of warfare'.

By contrast, Winston Churchill envisaged a radical new role for the RAF in this post-war world. *'The first duty of the RAF,'* he told Parliament in December 1919, *'is to garrison the British Empire.'* Churchill was an early and enthusiastic supporter of the RAF. He himself was a pilot, although almost universally judged to be a menace in the air.

There was also the small matter of the Army & the Royal Navy wanting their aeroplanes back.

ABOVE LEFT: The observer and pilot in a Handley Page bomber: the former in the nose, equipped with a Lewis gun on a Scarff ring

ABOVE RIGHT: Handley-Page bombers on a mission, Western Front, during World War I

OPP PAGE: Mechanics standing on the left wing of a Handley-Page bomber, checking the Aircraft before take off

'...Off with its head!'

Prime Minister Andrew Bonar Law, 1922

PLANES INTO PLOUGHSHARES

By 1920, the RAF had shrunk from a wartime figure of 300,000 personnel to just 3,280 officers and 25,000 in the ranks. The Women's RAF had been completely disbanded and combat squadrons reduced from 188 to a mere 29. The Ministry of Munitions set up a Disposal Board to get rid of literally tens of thousands of aeroplanes now surplus to requirements. Spare parts and landing fields were also sold off at knock down prices, both to raise cash and to make a political point.

As CAS, Trenchard still urgently needed to find some role for the fledgling RAF in a world at peace. He talked about developing an *'Air Spirit'*. He talked about the RAF being able to provide specialist services to the Army and Navy. He talked about influencing the future shape of warfare. He talked about deterrent. Nothing impressed the politicians. Then he followed Churchill's suggestion that the RAF could police the Empire on the cheap — and suddenly ears pricked up.

THE CHEAPEST WAR IN HISTORY

British Somaliland was hardly a jewel in the Empire's crown. It had virtually nothing in the way of natural resources to exploit and produced little except religious extremism and stringy camel meat. The British, who garrisoned the wretched place from Aden, were mainly concerned with stamping out slavery in the region. Since 1899, a religious zealot named Sayyid Mohammed Abdullah Hassan — or the *'Mad Mullah'* as the British referred to him — had been waging a holy war against British rule at the head of a Dervish army. Supported by the Ottoman Turks, he ruthlessly persecuted Somali Christians and any Muslims not of his sect. Successive attempts to deal with him by local British camel forces had failed over the past twenty years and now he was seen to be threatening Egypt to the north. To stop him, it was estimated that the British would need to send in three full divisions of troops — a hugely complex undertaking liable to cost the Treasury several million pounds.

LEFT: Illustration from 1901 titled 'The Defeat of the Mad Mullah in Somaliland' showing a British officer casually interrogating prisoners at the base camp at Burao

OPP. PAGE: Portrait of Lieutenant-General Aylmer Haldane in uniform

Lord Milner, the Colonial Secretary, approached Trenchard to see if the RAF could provide the answer instead. Trenchard assured him that it could and, very shortly after, twelve Airco DH.9A's designated Z Force were on their way to Somaliland aboard the carrier Ark Royal. Arriving in January 1920, they proceeded to strike Somali villages and the Mullah's hill forts, inflicting heavy losses on the Dervishes, who had never seen an aeroplane before and were often paralysed by superstitious dread. It was all over in three weeks. Many of the Mullah's family were killed in the bombing of his capital, Taleh, and the Mullah himself fled to the Ogaden region, where he then conveniently contracted Spanish Flu and died. It was a stunning victory for the Royal Air Force. They had rapidly achieved success with just 12 aircraft in a conflict that the Army had not managed to win in 20 years - and all for considerably less than £100,000. The intervention is now sometimes referred to as *'the cheapest war in history'*. Trenchard had proven his point and perhaps assured the future of the Royal Air Force.

IRAQ

At the end of the Great War, Britain and France had assumed control of large parts of the Middle East from the Ottoman Empire and now ran them as mandates. Almost immediately, both nations realised they had been handed a poisoned chalice. The entire region was riven with deep and intractable ethnic, tribal and religious divisions. Everybody hated everybody and had done so with murderous passion for untold centuries. Now, they hated their new *'masters'* too. In May 1920, Sunni and Shia put aside their divisions to rise up against the British. Thousands of Iraqis died in the fighting and more than 500 British and colonial troops were killed too. The revolt was put down, but the cost to the Treasury was in the tens of millions of pounds. After the conflict, Churchill received a communique from General Haldane, Commander-in-Chief in Baghdad, saying:

'Indeed, I now think that had I had sufficient aircraft last year I might have prevented the insurrection spreading from beyond the first incident at Rumaitha'.

At the 1921 Cairo Conference Winston Churchill, now Secretary of State for Air and the Colonies, handed over control of all British forces in Iraq to the RAF. Yet another insurgency was threatening Iraq and Churchill was hoping for the kind of cost-effective solution that the RAF had provided in Somaliland. Without the RAF, Churchill estimated that between 25,000 and 80,000 British and Indian troops would be needed to bring Iraq under control. With the RAF, no more

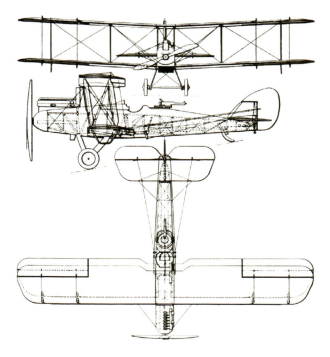

than 10,000 personnel would be required. The RAF Squadrons deployed to Iraq would be backed up by armoured car companies and battalions of Levies, rather than massed troops who could now be safely withdrawn.

The RAF officially took over operations in Iraq from 1 October 1921, with the formation of RAF Iraq Command under Air Vice Marshal Sir John Salmond. Eight RAF squadrons were deployed comprising de Havilland DH9s, Bristol Fighters and Vickers Vernon transports. Villages and tribes that proved difficult or threatening were simply bombed and for the large part pacified — and Britain did indeed save money. Military expenditure in Iraq dropped from £23m in 1921 to under £4m in 1925. The policy of 'Air Control' soon spread across Palestine, Arabia and the North West Frontier — huge stretches of land that were impossible for ground forces to ever police adequately.

PUBLIC PERCEPTIONS

Trenchard had effectively won government approval for the survival of the RAF by showing it could more than pay its way, but the public was another matter. For them, the Empire was very far away - unlike the horrors of recent war. To win over the public, Trenchard understood that the RAF could not be *'sold'* as a war

machine. It had to be useful in other ways as well as a source of pride.

Almost immediately after the war, the RAF began a postal service taking family letters out to the troops occupying Germany. RAF pilots and planes set new aviation records in distance, altitude and speed. Alcock and Brown made the first direct Atlantic crossing. Just a few weeks later, an RAF airship made the Atlantic crossing — twice. RAF aviators flew (with numerous stopovers) from Britain to Australia. RAF planes pioneered air routes throughout the Empire which would then become operated by civil aviation. The RAF even had its own, popular RAF Central Band, which was the first military band to play on the BBC and which still exists today. Not content with music to the ears, Trenchard also quickly came up with a feast for the eyes…

ABOVE LEFT: Brigadier-General John Maitland Salmond

ABOVE RIGHT: Airco DH.9 British First World War two seat bomber drawing

OPP. PAGE: Vickers Vernon in Palestine

OPP. PAGE INSET LEFT: De Havilland DH 9A, ER8733, in flight

OPP. PAGE INSET RIGHT: Bristol F.2

HEARTS AND MINDS AND HENDON

The RAF held its first 'Air Pageant' on 3 July 1920 at Hendon aerodrome to show off its aircraft and capabilities — and it was an instant sensation. Many more followed for the next two decades, and it was not uncommon for the RAF to devote 250 aircraft to the event. Stunt flying, mock dogfights and passes by massed formations wowed crowds of up to 150,000, as did set-piece mock bombing attacks on dummy targets which always culminated in a large and satisfying explosion. It's revealing that the 1922 poster promises the destruction of an *'eastern stronghold'* (i.e. Arabic), showcasing the RAF's new role in Iraq. The Arabs were referred to as the 'Wottnotts'. By 1926, Flight Magazine was describing the event as *'amongst the foremost of the functions of the London social season',* with the King and Queen, foreign royals, maharajas and much of Parliament in attendance.

ESPIRIT D'CORPS

As Trenchard laboured to win over the hearts of the public, behind the scenes he worked tirelessly to give the RAF its own living, beating heart. He had taken command of an organisation that was virtually a blank slate, whereas the Army and Navy enjoyed rich traditions going back many centuries. Trenchard felt deeply that his new force needed to create its own *'Air Spirit'* and sense of belonging as soon as possible — a state of mind that would be installed during training. Both the Army and Navy offered to provide training to new RAF recruits, but Trenchard wisely turned them down. He did not want his new airmen having their values instilled by rival services who still wanted to see the RAF broken up and returned to them.

The RAF Training College opened at Cranwell in Lincolnshire in February 1920. Despite being intended to train the officer elite of the RAF, it was a dump in the middle of nowhere consisting of corrugated iron huts set in often liquid mud (it would remain ghastly for almost a decade, until grand new, Wren-inspired college buildings were opened in 1929). New recruits found Cranwell very similar to their old public schools. Rugger was a must and new boys were hazed and humiliated. It even had its own pack of hounds for bothering the local wildlife. It recruited exclusively from the public schools and naturally Eton had its own dedicated liaison officer.

The mechanics and other lower ranks would be trained as apprentices at Halton Hall in Buckinghamshire. Harbouring secret dreams of one day being able to fly, here the children of the working classes came straggling in by bus or bicycle, with their few possessions wrapped up tightly by mum in crumpled brown paper tied with string. Few could afford suitcases — and even fewer would ever fly. Only three apprentices a year were allowed to transfer to Cranwell. In the first years, 5,000 boys applied for just 300 places. They called them *'Trenchard's Brats'* — and they were very much his.

THE AUXILIARY AIR FORCE

Despite recruiting through Cranwell and Halton, the RAF still could not find enough men to meet their needs — and Trenchard next appropriated the concept of the Army's Territorials. In 1925, the Auxiliary Air Force (AAF) was established, with different squadrons around the country offering pilots the opportunity to fly in their spare time on RAF types. These AAF Squadrons had a distinctly elitist air about them (one had to be of *'pure European stock'* to belong) and were not for the average man in the street. Trenchard himself said that belonging to an AAF squadron would be like acceptance into a *'good club'*. 601 Squadron earned the nickname *'The Millionaires Squadron'* after it was set up by Lord Edward Grosvenor. Only those in his lordship's social circle were allowed to join. While AAF squadrons sounded like the province of spoiled socialites, it has to be noted that, during the Battle of Britain, almost a quarter of Fighter Command pilots came from the AAF.

Additional fresh and bright young recruits would be lifted straight from the best universities. University Air Squadrons were established from 1925 onwards. Naturally, Oxford and Cambridge were the first choices. As with the AAF, the universities were to provide a good number of pilots for the Battle of Britain.

BRITISH AVIATION

By the end of the Great War, almost 2,000 British companies were involved in some way in aviation. Three years later, it would be difficult to find forty. Westland was forced to turn to manufacturing beer barrels just to survive. Others diversified into motor bikes or cars. Suddenly, there was no government money of any consequence, and little private demand to fill the void. The government was not interested (until mid-decade at least) in helping civil aviation. Let it *'fly by itself'* was the maxim. As a result, aircraft design in the 1920s changed very little. Better engines were developed, more as a point of pride than profit, and RAF's colonial role had an influence, but even the very latest warplanes were little more than refined versions of original Great War designs.

ABOVE: VIPs present at the founding ceremony for the new College Hall building at the RAF Cadet College, Cranwell. From left to right are: Unknown female (possibly Lady Trenchard), Lord Londonderry, Maud, Lady Hoare, Air Vice-Marshal F C Halahan - RAF College Commandant, Sir Samuel Hoare - Secretary of State for Air and Marshal of the RAF Sir Hugh Trenchard - Chief of the Air Staff

OPP. PAGE: A Royal Air Force pilot leans against his plane holding his monkey mascot, at the first Hendon Air Pageant

A GLORIOUS EXCEPTION

If there were any truly outstanding British aircraft of the times, they would have to be Reginald J. Mitchell's sleek and powerful Supermarine monoplane seaplanes which came to dominate the prestigious Schneider Trophy Race at the end of the decade. Trenchard had personally seen to it that RAF funds and resources went into Britain's 1927 entry, including the setting up of a High Speed Flight — for which he was roundly criticised. He was vindicated when British S.5s won 1st and 2nd place. Britain's S.6 won again in 1929. By the time of the next race, in 1931, the government had forbidden any funds being wasted on the race and it was only due to a generous private donation of £100,000 by Lady Houston that Britain was even able to enter. The Supermarine S.6B not only won, but established a new world air speed record of 380mph — at a time when the very best British fighter struggled to do 200 mph. More importantly, in just a few short years, the S.6B would evolve into the prototype of the Spitfire.

CIVIL WAR

Demands for the RAF to return air power to the Army and Royal Navy had flared up just before the turn of the decade. In December 1919, Trenchard had met with his chief antagonist, First Sea Lord Admiral Beatty, and told him, *'Air is one and indivisible'*. He asked Beatty for a year to prove his point and the admiral agreed. A year later, Beatty was still not convinced and so a series of government committees were set up to review RAF independence throughout the early 1920s. All came out in favour of an independent RAF. The RAF's continued existence was now assured, but some fudges had to be made. In 1924, the Fleet Air Arm of the RAF was formed — and the Admiralty were given at least partial control over the new body.

THE THREAT OF FRANCE

Throughout the 1920s, British politicians alternated between thinking with their hearts and their heads. Although seduced by utopian thoughts of a future without war, they nevertheless grasped that the world was still a very dangerous place and that Britain needed some form of defence.

At the start of the 1920s, the British government began to develop a fear of France. It had bounced back remarkably well after the war. There were concerns expressed that a French Air Force would find it easy and even convenient to bomb England. The numbers looked bad. The Times, in March 1922, reported that the French had 600 frontline warplanes. Britain, sadly, had just 40 aircraft to rise up against them should they hop the Channel.

Although Trenchard did not believe that the French had any evil intentions

on Britain, he was happy not to disabuse the politicians of their fears and stoked them for the benefit of the RAF, saying:

'…the air menace from France would be a grave danger in future years, if our relations with her become unsatisfactory'.

In 1923, the cabinet of Prime Minister Stanley Baldwin acknowledged the need to formulate the *'Air Defence of Great Britain'*, which would require 52 RAF squadrons with a first-line strength of 594 aircraft. Trenchard somewhat wilfully

interpreted this as meaning 17 fighter squadrons and 35 bomber squadrons allocated to the 'Independent Air Force' and the bomber deterrent. The 52 squadrons were meant to be formed as a matter of urgency, but deep rooted opposition on both ideological and financial grounds in successive governments impeded their progress. The RAF'S 52 Squadrons were not in place by the start of the 1930s as envisaged. They had officially been delayed until 1938.

GOODBYE

By 1928, Hugh Trenchard knew that he had assured the survival and future prospects of his beloved RAF and offered his resignation. He believed that the RAF was a young service and would best be served now by a younger man with fresh eyes and ideas. He himself was in his early 50s. Initially, Parliament refused his resignation and he would continue on his post as CAS until 1 January 1930.

ABOVE: Supermarine Rolls-Royce S6B seaplane

OPP. PAGE LEFT: RAF team for the Schneider Trophy race in 1929

OPP. PAGE RIGHT: Admiral Earl Beatty, HMN, Commander in Chief

On 6 July 1935, His Majesty King George V reviewed the Royal Air Force at Duxford and Mildenhall. 356 aircraft were presented for ground inspection at Mildenhall. Twenty squadrons then took part in a flypast. Every single aircraft that took part in the events was a biplane. The fighters — Bulldogs, Furys and Gloster Gauntlets — all biplanes. The bombers — Heyfoods, Harts, Audaxes and Demons — all biplanes. Even the very latest fighter aircraft, the Gloster F7/30, proudly laid out for His Majesty's close inspection, was a biplane. War with Nazi Germany was less than five years away.

A POOR START

As the decade turned, and Hugh Trenchard was replaced by Sir John Salmond as CAS, it was immediately obvious that — while Trenchard had achieved many of his aims in securing the future of the RAF - he had singularly failed to persuade the politicians to give it adequate funding. His compromise had been to lay down firm foundations for a small air force, but one which was flexible enough to be expanded rapidly if the need arose. He famously said:

'I have laid the foundation for a castle: if nobody builds anything bigger than a cottage on them, it will at least be a very good cottage.'

In 1930, the entire budget of the RAF — or 'Air Estimate' - was just £21 million. In 1931, it would be even less and by 1933 it had been reduced still further to £16.8 million. As a result, RAF front line aircraft were virtually obsolete. The pride of the Bomber Fleet, the Handley Page Heyford, introduced in 1933, struggled to fly at more than 100 mph. British aircraft manufacturers, still starved of any real investment from government, were concentrating on civil aviation instead. As a result, many civil aircraft could now significantly outperform their military counterparts.

Out in the furthest reaches of empire, pilots and crew lived in tents or the shabbiest of huts. Sanitation was often next to non-existent and RAF men were far more at risk from sickness than any hostile populace. Trenchard's Brats from Halton were asked to work mechanical miracles, keeping some planes flying only by cannibalising spare parts from other aircraft. Warplanes would often have to take off and land on bald metal wheel rims as there were no tyres available. For the men keeping the near-wrecks flying, pay was the lowest it has ever been and both accommodation and canteen food — even back in Blighty - was little short of filthy and disgusting for anyone below officer class.

But times were changing — and would force a change in political thinking. The question would become, could the RAF be modernised and expanded in time?

THE TWO MINDS OF MR STANLEY BALDWIN

At the start of the 1930s, Stanley Baldwin — then Lord President of the Council in Ramsay MacDonald's National Coalition government - was firmly against the growth of military force. He held to Sir Edward Grey's famous 1925 statement that *'great armaments lead inevitably to war.'*

In January 1932, Japanese bombers unleashed a hail of bombs against the Chinese city of Shanghai. It was a slaughter. Within just days, the cinema newsreels brought terrifying film of the raid to the West. Audiences watched the city burn, enveloped in thick black smoke. They saw vast columns of refugees trying to flee the city — and everywhere there were bodies. The future flickered on every cinema screen. *'Shanghai is a nightmare,'* Baldwin confessed.

The bombing of Shanghai essentially pulled Baldwin in two directions. His idealistic instinct was to press for the scrapping of the world's bomber fleets — but the realist in him was alarmed by the vulnerability of Britain to air attack. The Geneva Disarmament Conference, at which Baldwin had been pushing for *'air disarmament'*, started to fall apart in 1933 when the German delegation pulled out. That same month, Germany withdrew from the League of Nations, and Baldwin started to advocate that Britain should have an air force equal to any future hostile nation. In this, he still believed that the RAF would act as a successful deterrent to war and not a shot would ever be fired nor a single bomb dropped. After all, the Nazis were rational men.

FROM COTTAGE TO CASTLE

The first Royal Air Force Expansion Scheme, Scheme A, would expand the RAF to 111 front-line squadrons at home and abroad, totalling 1,252 aircraft. A further 213 aircraft would comprise sixteen Fleet Air Arm squadrons under RAF control. This was intended to be achieved by the end of the decade. Progress was, in practice, painfully slow at least at first, with both lack of government will and not inconsiderable opposition from the public and

pacifist elements. There was also considerable consternation at the Treasury when they learned that any new and improved fighter aircraft might cost as much as £20,000 each — and a good new bomber £100,000. Such an outlay was surely unthinkable in a world still dedicated to peace and mired in an economic depression.

Stanley Baldwin made a potentially fatal error during 1934 and 1935 by believing reports about the true size of the Luftwaffe. For the longest time, he was convinced that the RAF outnumbered German planes almost two to one. He was profoundly shocked when it was finally revealed in May 1935 that the Luftwaffe already possessed some 370 more planes than the RAF. The Nazis had been training pilots in secret and building civilian aircraft that could be easily converted to military types. The RAF would require an extra 1,400 aircraft above existing growth estimates just to keep pace. Even if the 1,400 were delivered, the German aircraft industry had the capacity now to build far, far more over the time period. In quick response, the government agreed to drastically expand the Home Defence portion of the RAF to 1,512 aircraft, comprising 840 bombers and 420 fighter aircraft. 2,500 extra pilots would be recruited and the number of RAF bases increased from 52 to 138. To achieve this, the Treasury initially granted just an extra £5,500,000.

'I was wrong in my estimate of the future. There I was completely wrong,' Baldwin confessed to Parliament.

'THE BOMBER WILL ALWAYS GET THROUGH'

Throughout the 1930s, one of the foremost questions was what sort of air force should the RAF be. In November 1932, following the Japanese terror bombings

RIGHT: Stanley Baldwin

of Chinese cities, Baldwin used the infamous phrase *'the bomber will always get through'* in Parliament, crystallizing the predominant thinking of the day. He said:

'I think it as well for the man in the street to realize that there is no power on earth that prevents him from being bombed. Whatever people may tell him, the bomber will always get through…the only defence is offence, which means that you will have to kill more women and children more quickly than the enemy if you want to save yourselves.'

Bombers then would decide any future war. Swatting fighters aside like gnats, they would obliterate the great cities of Europe with bombs and clouds of poison gas. Whole populations would be wiped out in a *'knockout blow'*, probably within scant days of any outbreak of hostilities. Conventional thinking turned towards Trenchard's idea of the 'Independent Air Force'

bomber deterrent and against fighter aircraft.

Despite this, public opinion still largely favoured the fighter. They wanted the reassurance of some opposition to bombers over their cities, just as they had demanded during the Great War. The government looked for a satisfying compromise. Maybe the answer to the bomber threat was not the fighter. Maybe it was a Death Ray. An Aeronautical Research Committee was set up comprised of scientists whose job it was to create a *'death ray'* which would scorch enemy bombers from the skies. The *'death ray'* proved a nonsense — but from this scientists developed the idea of Radio Direction Finding — or radar. Consequently, 20 *'Chain Home'* radar stations were established around Britain's coastline, each capable of seeing approaching aircraft from as much as 100 miles away. They would of course play a pivotal role in the Battle of Britain yet to come.

HEAVY BOMBERS

Still largely convinced that it was the bomber that would win any future war, the Air Ministry issued new specifications for metal *'heavy'* monoplane bombers in 1936. From this came the Short Stirling, the Handley Page HP 56 and the Avro Manchester. The first Stirling flew in May 1939, but unfortunately crashed and did not join RAF service until August 1940, when 7 Squadron received their first aircraft. The HP56 prototype flew first in 1939 and the first aircraft were supplied to 35 Squadron in November 1940. The HP56 became the Halifax. Intended initially as a twin engine bomber, the Avro Manchester's design caused much concern even after it entered service in November 1940.

FAITH IN FIGHTERS

Fortunately for the government, the British aviation industry had shown more foresight than the politicians and had been working on fighter designs in private. They were aided in this — somewhat unofficially — by Squadron Leader Ralph Sorley, Head of the Operational Requirements Section of the Air Ministry who kept the lines of communication open and came up with a *'wish list'* for a new fighter. Out of this came not one but two of the finest fighter aircraft of the era…

MAIN IMAGE: Avro Manchester, 2RR Vulture

THE HAWKER HURRICANE

Essentially designed as a monoplane successor to the Hawker Fury by its Chief Designer Sydney Camm, the Hawker Hurricane was the world's first fighter armed with eight machine guns and was capable of speeds of over 300 mph. In 1936, the Air Ministry placed an initial order for 600 Hurricanes and the fighter first entered service with 111 Squadron the following year. Being based on Depression-era production values, it was easy to build and relatively cheap to maintain and service.

Flying with its chief rival the Spitfire during the Battle of Britain, the Hurricane claimed 60% of all *'kills'*. While being able to stand up to the Me.109, it was inferior in some respects and it was preferred practice to vector it against bomber formations while Spitfires dealt with the fighter escorts.
14,583 were built during the seven years of its production, including many variants designed for night fighting, tropical service, ground attack and service at sea.

MAIN IMAGE: Hawker Hurricane

BELOW LEFT: Line drawing of a British WWII Hawker Hurricane Mk.I

OPP. PAGE LEFT: Sydney Camm, 1917

OPP. PAGE MIDDLE / RIGHT: Hawker employees Winnie Bennett, Dolly Bennett, Florence Simpson and a colleague at work on the production of Hurricane fighter aircraft at a factory in Britain, in 1942

THE SUPERMARINE SPITFIRE

The Spitfire was very much the vision of R.J. Mitchell, based on his Schneider Trophy-winning seaplane monoplane designs. The Spitfire prototype first flew on March 1936. On landing its test pilot, Captain Joseph 'Mutt' Summers famously said, 'Don't touch anything.' In June 1936, the Air Ministry placed an initial order for 310 fighters. Weeks later, it debuted at the 1936 RAF Hendon Air Display.

Manufacturing problems meant that the first models did not come off the production line until the summer of 1938. 19 Squadron at Duxford received their first Spitfires to replace their obsolete Gauntlet biplanes that August, but they remained in relatively short supply well into 1940. The Spitfire proved it was a thoroughbred fighter during the Battle of Britain, where in many critical respects it out-performed the Me.109, especially at higher altitude. Proportionately, it suffered fewer casualties than the Hurricane and achieved a higher 'victory to loss' ratio.

Throughout the rest of the war, the Spitfire was constantly refined and improved to meet evolving German threats such as the Fw.190 fighter. It served in every significant theatre, and its critical role as one of the best photo reconnaissance aircraft of the war is often overlooked. It was also the only British fighter to remain in production throughout the war and over 22,000 were built. Incredibly, when the Spitfire F24 was introduced in 1946, it could still out-perform all jet aircraft then in service.

Spitfires flew their last operational combat sortie with the RAF in January 1951 during the Malayan Emergency.

MAIN IMAGE: Spitfire in flight

OPP. PAGE BOTTOM RIGHT: Reginald Joseph Mitchell

OPP. PAGE LEFT: Spitfires and Lancaster Bombers on the runway at Castle Bromwich 1944

OPP. PAGE MIDDLE: A civilian storewoman holds up spare panels for Supermarine Spitfires, stored at No 25 Maintenance Unit, Hartlebury, Worcestershire

OPP. PAGE RIGHT: Two RAF fitters at work on the Rolls Royce Merlin engine of a Supermarine Spitfire, beneath the bomb bay of a Handley Page Halifax converted for the purpose of carrying a Spitfire fuselage

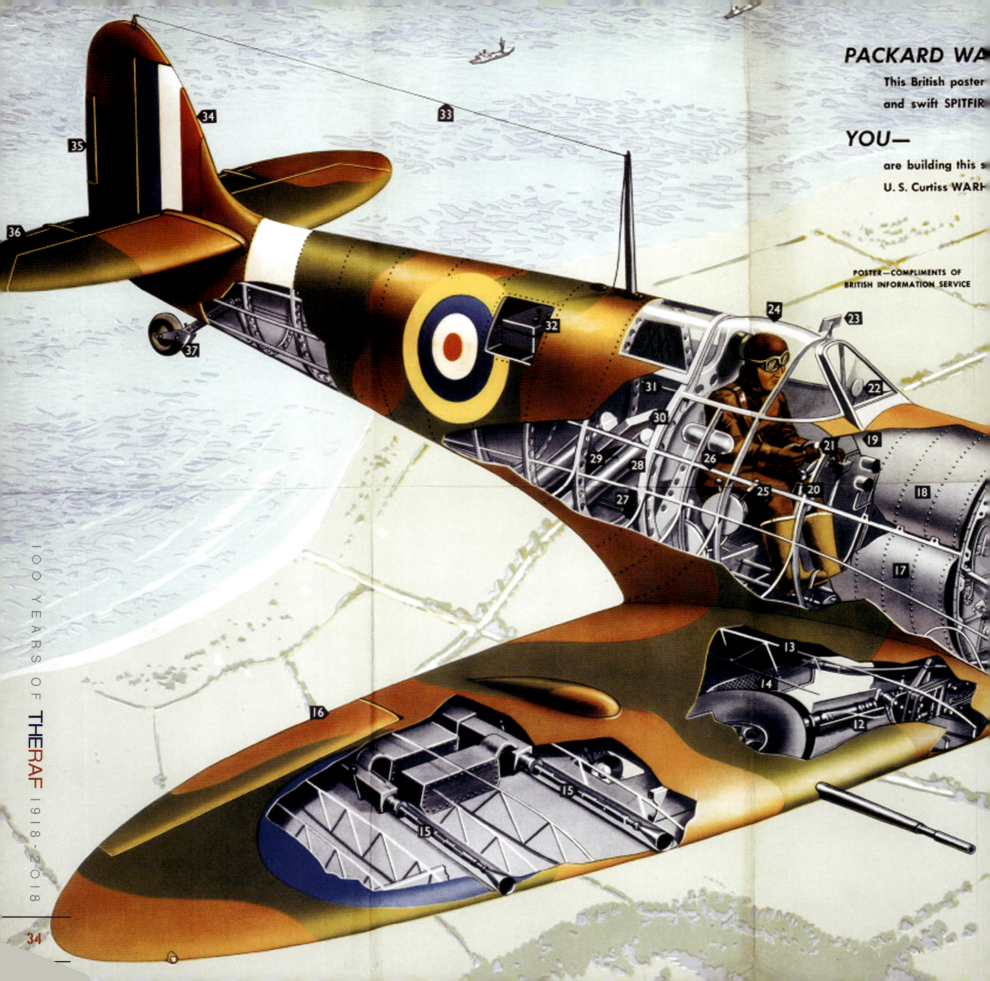

RKERS—

tricate construction of the deadly
by a Rolls-Royce aircraft engine.

sted engine for the lightning-fast
mparable English fighting planes.

Work to Win

Committee

BRITAIN'S NEW "SPITFIRE"

With an even more powerful Rolls-Royce
erlin" engine, the "Spitfire" enters the lists again,
engined and re-armed. It is now armed with two
non and four machine guns. The official speed
Spitfire I" was over 366 m.p.h. at 18,500 feet.
rate of initial climb was 2,300 feet per minute.
nts in "Spitfire" design are its all-metal
struction, stressed metal covering, outwards

retracting undercarriage. Fixed tail wheel, radiator
under starboard wing, are other points. Wing-
span is 36 feet 10 inches ; height, 11 feet 5 inches.
The Supermarine "Spitfire I" was evolved from
the seaplane which won the Schneider Trophy, for
the third successive time and outright in 1931.
"Achtung Schpitfeuer" are still the last words many
a Nazi airman will hear.

ETAL-COVERED WINGS	13 METAL RIBS	24 SLIDING HOOD
ANNON	14 RADIATOR	25 UNDERCARRIAGE CONTROL HANDLE
HREE-BLADED CONSTANT-SPEED	15 MACHINE GUNS	26 LONGERON
AIR SCREW	16 AILERON	27 BATTERY BOX
ANK	17 LOWER FUEL TANK	*Total Fuel Load*	28 PARACHUTE FLARE
OLLS-ROYCE "MERLIN" ENGINE	18 UPPER FUEL TANK	*85 Gallons*	29 METAL RIBS
XHAUSTS	19 INSTRUMENT PANEL	30 DITTY BOX
L TANK	20 CONTROL LEVER	31 STRINGER
NGINE BEARERS	21 FIRING TRIGGER	32 RADIO
ARBURETTOR AIR INTAKE	22 GUN SIGHT	33 AERIAL
UPERCHARGER	23 MIRROR	34 FIN
IREPROOF BULKHEAD		35 RUDDER
ETRACTED UNDERCARRIAGE	LENGTH 29 ft. 11 in.	36 ELEVATORS
(STARBOARD)	SPAN OF PLANES 36 ft. 10 in.	37 TAIL WHEEL

EXPANSION SCHEME F

By 1936, it was obvious that the Nazis would not be deterred by numbers. Combat power in the air would be the deciding factor. Expansion Scheme F, approved by the government in February 1936, drastically increased the number of new aircraft for the RAF to 8,000. More importantly, those aircraft would be the latest types available — fighters like the Hurricane and Spitfire and bombers including the Fairey Battle, Blenheim, Hampden, Wellesley, Whitley and Wellington.

IN COMMAND

In July 1936, the Air Defence of Great Britain Command was scrapped and replaced with four new organisations — Bomber Command, Fighter Command, Coastal Command and Training Command. The reorganisation came in response to the RAF's now rapid expansion — and the need to be prepared for war. Additionally, there were five overseas Commands — Mediterranean, Aden, Middle East, India and Far East.

THE FLEET AIR ARM

On July 30 1937, Prime Minister Neville Chamberlain announced the Royal Navy would take complete control of the Fleet Air Arm from the RAF. It was a victory of sorts for the Admiralty, after almost 20 years of lobbying to possess their own air force. They were none too pleased that the RAF would keep RAF Coastal Command, but accepted it with semi-good grace.

EXPANSION SCHEME L

Even with a better political will, Expansion Scheme F still failed to meet its objectives by 1938. Only 4,500 aircraft had been delivered, and getting only the latest and best aircraft types proved exceptionally difficult to an aviation industry struggling now to gear up to meet demand.

RIGHT: Cut-out drawing of a Spitfire

The Style for You
is Air Force Blue!

—JOIN THE WAAF

In 1938, against the backdrop of the Nazi annexing of Austria, Expansion Scheme L replaced F. Now 12,000 new aircraft were wanted instead of 8,000. Suddenly financial considerations were dropped and a new, wartime thinking predominated. Once again though, the British aircraft industry found it difficult to meet the demand after so many *'lean years'*.

STANDING READY

By 1939, the RAF stood ready to meet the Nazi threat — or as ready as it could be. It could boast 157 squadrons comprising almost 2,000 warplanes (around half the strength of the Luftwaffe). The *'Air Estimate'* for the RAF had ballooned to £200 million. New training schools had opened and the Women's Auxiliary Air Force (WAAF) had been established to free up men for other duties. Further boosting personnel was the RAF Volunteer Reserve, set up in 1936 by the Director of Training at the Air Ministry, Commodore Arthur Tedder. Realising that class distinctions were keeping the number of recruits low, he proposed that the RAF needed to be open *'…to the whole middle class (and) the complete range of the output of the public and secondary schools'*. Men between the ages of 18 to 25 could learn to fly and be paid £25 a year. The response was enormous. By the outbreak of war, there were 10,000 RAFVR men standing ready and 310 RAFVR pilots were already flying with Fighter Command.

The RAF now had 270 Spitfires and 400 Hurricanes in service, but much of its fighter strength was still comprised of outdated aircraft like the Gloster Gladiator and Boulton Paul Defiant. The bigger bombers were not yet ready and RAF Bomber Command would be forced to field less capable, lighter aircraft when war came, including the Fairey Battle, Whitley, Blenheim and Hampden.

WAR

When war was declared on Germany on 3 September 1939, the air raid sirens sounded — but it was a false alarm. The skies over London were empty. The predicted mass bomber fleets never materialised.

On that first day, Hampden bombers did set out to bomb German ships — but failed to find them. A Blenheim on reconnaissance duties located several warships, but the aircraft wireless set failed. The next day, Blenheims and Wellingtons set out to bomb German ships at two different ports. Their *'General Purpose'* bombs did next to no damage and seven aircraft were lost. Twenty four men died, and the greatest damage to the cruiser Emden was caused by a stricken Blenheim crashing into it. One of the RAF bombers accidentally bombed Denmark.

After the failure of the raid, bomber missions were mostly restricted to leaflet dropping until 14 December, when 43 bombers were despatched against German shipping. Five were shot down for no tangible results. On the 18th, twenty four Wellingtons took off to attack shipping in the port of Wilhelmshaven — and were intercepted by Luftwaffe Me.110s. Twelve RAF bombers — half the entire force — were shot down inside thirty minutes. Until now, it had been believed that bombers flying in a tight formation could put up enough gunfire to destroy or deter attacking fighters. Reality proved otherwise. The bomber, it seemed, would not always get through after all.

During this time, RAF Coastal Command launched missions against German U-boats, but many of their aircraft were obsolete and they too found their GP bombs inadequate for the task. In return, the eight German U-boats stationed in the eastern Atlantic sank over 150,000 tons of shipping in just the first three weeks of the war. Britain depended on imports to survive — and the Nazi strategy was to blockade the sea lanes and bring the nation to heel.

It was not an auspicious start.

TOP LEFT: 'The Style for You is Air Force Blue!' was a recruitment booklet produced for the WAAF. Describing potential recruits as 'partners in victory'

BOTTOM 4 IMAGES L–R: 3 Fairey Battle Mk1s fly in formation; Parachute troops jump from a Whitley bomber during a demonstration for the King near Windsor; Bristol Blenheim; Loading bombs onto a World War II Handley Page Hampden

THE NORWEGIAN CAMPAIGN

On 9 April 1940, the Germans invaded Norway. Of all the places the RAF had envisaged fighting, Scandinavia had never been a serious consideration.

Bomber Command fared little better than it had in the opening days of the war. Twelve Hampdens attacking German shipping in daylight met German fighters — and half the bombers were lost. Bomber Command then shifted to night-only missions, attacking Norwegian airfields seized by the Germans. All the same problems were evident. The aircraft were just not good enough, and nor were their bombs and bomb aiming equipment. Without fighter escorts, bomber formations fell easy prey to German fighters. Navigation was also a serious issue — and problems were only compounded when

the bombers were being forced to fly by night. More often than not, Bomber Command couldn't find the target and if they did, they could only inflict minor damage — all the while being cut to pieces by anti-aircraft guns and German interceptors. Norway was lost but there were now greater concerns…

BLITZKRIEG

RAF warplanes had flown to bases in France almost as soon as war was declared. There they sat. The contribution of the RAF to Allied strength in France was divided into two. The Advanced Air Striking Force comprised in May 1940 ten squadrons of daylight bombers, principally Bristol Blenheims and Fairey Battles. The Air Component Section on the other hand was

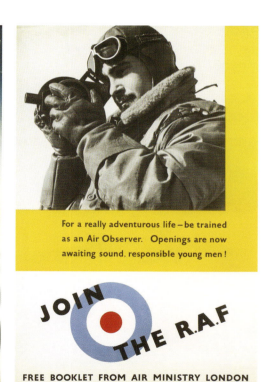

considered an integral part of the BEF and comprised ten squadrons of Hurricane fighters plus four Blenheim bomber squadrons and five squadrons of Lysander reconnaissance aircraft.

On 10 May 1940, German forces struck France as well as Belgium, Holland and Luxembourg. RAF airfields on the continent were bombed immediately, and Hurricanes went up after the raiding bombers to defend their airstrips. In retaliation for German hostility, 100 RAF bombers set out from England to bomb the Ruhr, but only one in four planes even claimed to have spotted their targets. Wedded as they were to the twin ideas of Home Defence and an offensive bomber force, the RAF had not fully thought through the idea of close air support, unlike the Luftwaffe for which it was one of its main functions, and so the Germans enjoyed a tactical advantage on the ground from the start.

Fairey Battles and Bristol Blenheims launched attacks against bridges in northern Belgium to slow the German advance — but the raids were a disaster. The slow-moving Fairey Battles in particular, forced to fly low because of lack of air cover, were shot to pieces by ground fire. In one raid over Luxembourg, seven out of eight Battles were lost. Of the nine Bristol Blenheims from 139 Squadron that set out to strike German columns near Maastricht in Holland, only two returned home. Five Fairey Battles from 12 Squadron were sent after the two surviving strategic bridges over the Albert Canal. They were all shot down. One bridge was destroyed only after a stricken Fairey Battle, flown by Flight Leader Donald *'Judy'* Garland, crashed right into it (The pilot and observer both received posthumous Victoria Crosses). In only three days, operational strength of RAF day bombers fell from 135 to just 72 aircraft.

Further disaster was to follow. There was one last chance to stop the Germans at Sedan. French and British aircraft made desperate, low level attempts to knock out the pontoon bridge German engineers had thrown across the Meuse. They faced a gauntlet of 303 anti-aircraft guns as they came in and it was a slaughter. 27 raids were launched during

the day. Every one failed. In just one day, the RAF lost forty more of their remaining bombers to murderous flak and German fighter cover. Air Officer Commanding-in-Chief British Air Forces in France, Air Marshal Sir Arthur Barratt, is said to have openly wept when he saw the casualty figures.

By 19 May, it was agreed that what was left of the BEF's RAF Component would leave their bases in France and return home to England. 120 damaged Hurricane fighters had to be abandoned and destroyed on their French fields. Only 66 planes made it home. Back on the continent, surviving British Army units fell back to the

LEFT: RAF recruitment posters

ABOVE: Air Marshal Sir Arthur Barratt

port of Dunkirk to await evacuation by sea. The RAF were severely stretched when it came to providing cover. Some 200 aircraft were made available, up against 300 German bombers and 550 fighters. The Spitfires and Hurricanes had to fly out from England, leaving them with only enough fuel for perhaps 20 minutes over Dunkirk — and they had to rely on visually spotting enemy formations before they could attack.

RAF losses in the Blitzkrieg were ferocious. In just two months, the RAF had lost 959 aircraft to the Luftwaffe's 1,284. Particularly alarming were the sheer number of pilots and crew lost in the fighting — 320 either dead or missing and a further 115 taken prisoner. They would be desperately missed when the inevitable German invasion of Britain began.

THE WAR AT SEA

From the start of the Second World War, the principal work of Coastal Command was to protect coastal waters and reconnoitre the North Sea for any German warship raiders. The Atlantic was very much the territory of the Royal Navy and the Fleet Air Arm. With the exception of the Sunderland and Hudson, few Coastal Command aircraft had the range to venture much further anyway. With priority given to Fighter and Bomber Command, Coastal Command was regarded as the *'Cinderella Service'* and got few new aircraft.

Between January and July 1940, Coastal Command's 500 aircraft between them sank just two U-boats, and then only with a great deal of assistance from the Navy. During the rest of 1940, they succeeded only in damaging two further German submarines. Meanwhile, in the second half of 1940 alone, almost 1,200 Allied ships were sunk.

'The gratitude of every home in our Island, in our Empire, and indeed throughout the world, except in the abodes of the guilty, goes out to the British airmen who, undaunted by odds, unwearied in their constant challenge and mortal danger, are turning the tide of the World War by their prowess and by their devotion. Never in the field of human conflict was so much owed by so many to so few.'

Prime Minister Winston Churchill, 20 August 1940.

RIGHT: A Sergeant bomb-aimer and photographer on board a Lockheed Hudson Mark I of No. 269 Squadron RAF at Wick, Caithness, demonstrates the use of a hand-held Type F.24 aerial camera from a port side window

THE BATTLE OF BRITAIN

The Battle of Britain began in the summer of 1940 with German raids on shipping in the Channel and southern ports as a prelude to invasion. 3,500 aircraft of the Luftwaffe faced off against just 700 RAF Fighters. Opposition from RAF Fighter Command was spirited and effective, but costly. Many irreplaceable pilots were lost when they were shot down over the sea. At the same time, the Luftwaffe used massed formations of bombers as bait, trying to tempt the RAF up for one enormous — and decisive — aerial battle. The RAF wisely refused to play the German's game, intercepting only with small numbers of fighters on the instructions of the Head of Fighter Command, Air Chief Marshal Hugh Dowding.

In mid-August, the Luftwaffe switched targets. Now they went after Britain's chain of radar stations, RAF air bases and aircraft factories throughout the south east. This had a far more damaging effect on the RAF. Between 8 and 16 August, Fighter Command lost 183 fighters shot down and a further thirty destroyed on the ground. 154 pilots were killed. The RAF simply could not afford these losses and had little more than a month's reserve of men and machines to call upon. The Luftwaffe continued to apply the pressure through late August, sometimes flying well over 1,000 sorties a day. It was only when a German bomber crew became lost and accidentally bombed London on the night of 24/25 August that things changed — considerably for the better. Churchill ordered RAF Bomber Command to bomb German cities in retaliation — infuriating Hitler.

Almost immediately, the Luftwaffe turned their attention away from RAF Stations and began a massive bombing assault on London itself. On 7 September, 900 German bombers and fighters swarmed towards London. It was a daylight raid the likes of which Britain had never known and over 300 RAF fighters rose to meet them. Both sides suffered heavy losses, and London's East End took the brunt of the bombing. Day after day, more massed raids were launched and met hard. On 15 September the Luftwaffe lost 50 aircraft over Southern England. They could not continue to sustain such losses — in excess of 1400 aircraft since July. Any hope of a successful invasion of Britain was finished, and all plans were cancelled on 12 October. From now on, the Luftwaffe would only come by night. The Battle of Britain had been won — but now The Blitz had begun.

MAIN IMAGE: RAF Scramble! Fighter Pilots race to their aircraft

BELOW LEFT: Observer Corps aircraft spotter on the roof of a building in London during the Battle of Britain, with St. Paul's Cathedral in the background

BELOW RIGHT: Interior of RAF Fighter Command's Sector 'G' Operations Room at Duxford, Cambridgeshire, September 1940

FIGHTING THE BLITZ

Fighter Command had little to throw at the night bomber fleets. The British radar system was not geared to cover the skies over Britain and the Observer Corps couldn't see the enemy at night. The first RAF aircraft used as night interceptors were Blenheims and Boulton Paul Defiants — the latter now regarded as next to obsolete after suffering crippling losses over France and during the Battle of Britain. Hurricanes and Spitfires shortly joined in, but had little more luck in even being able to find the German raiders in darkness. Things improved by 1941, with the introduction of Beaufighters armed with four 20mm cannon (as well as six machine guns), cannon-firing Spitfires and a top secret device called the Mark IV Air Interceptor Radar which could be carried on board night fighters. German bomber losses over Britain escalated rapidly.

MIDDLE EAST COMMAND

In June 1940, when the Italians declared war on Britain, RAF Middle East Command consisted of 29 squadrons comprising some 300 aircraft — much of which were long obsolete biplanes, apart from some Blenheims and Gladiators, which were at least part obsolete. With this meagre force, Air Chief Marshal Sir Arthur Longmore was supposed to cover everything from the Persian Gulf to Egypt to East Africa and north to the Balkans.

Despite this, what little Longmore had still proved considerably superior to

the Italian Air Force. They were busy supporting Wavell's forces in fending off an Italian thrust towards Egypt in October 1940, when the Italians also decided to invade Greece. Longmore was ordered to send his best aircraft — aircraft he couldn't spare — to Greece to show support. Despite a distinctly lacklustre showing by the Greek Air Force, RAF planes took a fearsome toll on the enemy with the Gladiators of 80 Squadron claiming 42 Italian aircraft destroyed by December 1940.

MALTA

The Italian Air Force began attacking the strategically vital Mediterranean island the day after they declared war. Defending the island were just four Fleet Air Arm Gloster Gladiators. A few Hurricanes were rushed to the island and a force of only ten aircraft held out until for almost two months until

OPP. PAGE: Flight Lieutenant Walter 'Farmer' Lawson, of No 19 Squadron, photographed in his flying kit at Fowlmere, late September 1940

ABOVE LEFT: A Bristol Blenheim about to touch down on a rough landing ground in Greece, 1941

ABOVE RIGHT: A Vickers Wellington DWI (Directional Wireless Installation) on the ground at Ismailia, Egypt

on 2 August twelve more Hurricanes were flown in off the carrier Argus to reinforce them. They became RAF 261 Squadron and were joined by the end of the year by the Wellingtons of 148 Squadron. More Hurricanes would soon join them to form 185 Squadron, defending the island almost daily during what amounted to a siege through the first six months of 1941. It was only when Hitler called much of his Mediterranean strength north to join in the invasion of Russia that the pressure finally eased. The RAF forces on Malta could now fly offensively against Axis supply ships — and sank 90,000 tons of enemy shipping in the last six months of 1941.

WAR IN THE MEDITERRANEAN

By the start of 1941, troops supported by RAF Middle East Command aircraft had blunted the Italian advance on Egypt and were fully on the offensive. Even the Wellingtons on Malta were drafted in to blitz the enemy as they retreated. New demands from Greece however meant that Longmore had to send further squadrons north, including irreplaceable newly-arrived Hurricanes. In March 1941, the Germans joined the Italians in Greece and RAF fighters found themselves facing 20-1 odds.. The following month, just seven surviving RAF fighters limped away to Crete as the Axis forces overwhelmed Greece. All other surviving RAF aircraft and personnel were evacuated to Crete, which was promptly invaded by the Germans on 20 May. There was no way that the 24 RAF aircraft evacuated to the island could

take on 650 Luftwaffe fighters and bombers…

Back in North Africa, over 100 Luftwaffe aircraft flew in to Tripoli to buttress the almost-defeated Italians from February 1941. The Allies were swiftly driven all the way back to Egypt, with the Axis enjoying overwhelming air superiority. The great push back was to come at the end of the year with 'Operation Crusader'. Air Marshal Arthur Tedder had assumed command from Longmore and what was now designated the Western Desert Air Force could throw no less than 37 Squadrons into the attack with fighters including Hurricanes, Martlets, Beaufighters and the American-built Tomahawk. New tactics were being employed, with the WDAS providing close air support for the advancing 8th Army while bombers went after Axis supply lines on land and at sea. By December, the Allies had won back virtually all the territory they had lost and the RAF had achieved some significant aerial superiority over great swathes of territory. There was little time to enjoy the victory. Tedder was told that his air force would once again have to be broken up with significant portions rushed to the Far East. WDAF held its gains for barely a month.

RAF FERRY COMMAND

RAF Ferry Command was set up on 20 July 1941, mostly to fly badly needed new warplanes from overseas to RAF bases in England. The pilots — some 3,500 in total — were all civilians. They flew without uniform, without

armaments — and without insurance. 9,442 aircraft out of 10,000 were successfully delivered by RAF Ferry Command, often across the Atlantic. Before RAF Ferry Command, losses of inbound aircraft had been around 50%. Over 500 members of the Command were lost before it became RAF Transport Command.

U-BOAT WAR

At the beginning of 1941, RAF Coastal Command had just 23 squadrons — a mixture of flying boats like the Sunderland and land-based warplanes including Wellingtons, Ansons, Hudsons and new Beaufort torpedo bombers.

That year, the U-boat menace intensified with the establishing of submarine pens in occupied Norway and France. Half a million tons of Allied ships went down every single month during the first six months of 1941. The U-boats were joined in 1941 by the battleships Gneisenau, Scharnhorst and Admiral von Sheer which had all managed to break out into the Atlantic and were now raiding shipping. The losses were clearly unsustainable — but things were finally changing in favour of Coastal Command..

New inventions like the Air-to-surface vessel (ASV) radar and then the Leigh Searchlight provided hope, with Coastal Command now better able to detect U-boats recharging their batteries on the surface at night. By Mid-1941, half of Coastal Command's aircraft had ASV on board and new airborne depth charges were starting to take a mounting toll on enemy submarines. Coastal Command had grown to a strength of 40 squadrons, with some flying American Liberator bombers and Catalina flying boats. Others had been equipped with the new Bristol Beaufighter with its four 20mm nose cannons and six machine guns which packed a considerable punch.

OPP. PAGE LEFT: 40 Squadron RAF Wellington at Gibraltar

OPP. PAGE RIGHT: Five Malta-based pilots sitting in front of two fighter aircraft at Luqa. Behind them is a Supermarine Spitfire Mark VC, BR498 'PP-H', parked in front of a Bristol Beaufighter of No. 272 Squadron RAF

RIGHT: Leigh Light used for spotting U-boats on the surface at night fitted to a Liberator aircraft of Royal Air Force Coastal Command

DE HAVILLAND MOSQUITO

'The Wooden Wonder', as the Mosquito was cheerfully nicknamed, was originally conceived and designed as a fast bomber. Indeed, as it first rolled off the production lines in 1941, it was then one of the fastest aircraft in the world. It initially carried no guns or cannon, as the designers believed it could simply outrun any trouble.

Apart from its wooden construction and speed coupled with a long range, what really set the Mosquito apart was how many different roles it could be adapted to within the RAF. It could bomb at high or ultra-low altitudes, or be adapted to serve as both a night or day fighter. It was perfect for photo reconnaissance and equally suited to attacking enemy shipping or surfaced U-boats with bombs, machine guns, rockets or nose-mounted cannon. 7,781 aircraft were built in all, with no less than 27 variants.

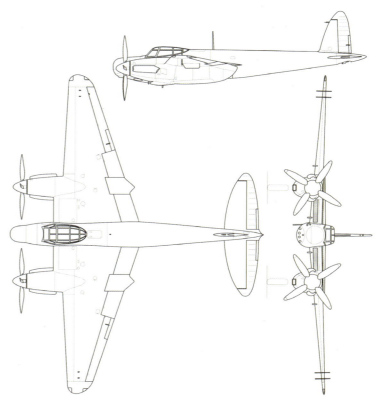

MAIN IMAGE: De Havilland Mosquito in flight

RIGHT: Line drawing of De Havilland Mosquito

OPP. PAGE T-B: RAF Mosquitos of No. 4 Squadron; A de Havilland Mosquito on the ground with a RAE-Vickers rocket model in place below the fuselage; Loading bombs onto De Havilland Mosquito; A passenger travelling in the bomb bay of a De Havilland Mosquito of BOAC, on the fast freight service between Leuchars, Fife and Stockholm, Sweden

BREATHING SPACE

In the summer of 1941, the Germans launched Operation Barbarossa — their planned invasion of Soviet Russia — and every aircraft was needed to support their panzers. Consequently, most of the bombers Goering had used for the Blitz were now deployed to the east and air raids on Britain eased up considerably.

With the pressure now off of Fighter Command, attention focused on Bomber Command to strike back. The problem was that Bomber Command was still not yet up to strength. The heavy bombers were few, training was behind schedule, and maintenance considerations were such that probably only

400 of the RAF's 1,000 bombers could be up and flying on any given night. Navigation was a problem too. Cologne was attacked by RAF Bomber Command 33 times between June 1941 and February 1942. Only one in every six bombs dropped actually hit the city. It was estimated that just one out every three crews claiming a direct hit had even come within five miles of target. Over the Ruhr, this problem stretched to an astounding one in ten.

In 1941, RAF Bomber Command only managed to drop 31,704 tons of bombs — the vast majority of which missed — for the loss of over 1,000 aircraft and 4,000 men killed or taken prisoner. Something had to change.

WAR IN THE FAR EAST

At the time of Pearl Harbor in December 1941, RAF Far East Command had only 181 RAF aircraft capable of flying in the whole theatre. The war at home meant that few resources could be spared. When war came, the RAF were simply overwhelmed by the Japanese. Old Vildebeest biplanes and Brewster Buffalo fighters, supported by pitifully few but more modern Hurricanes and Blenheims were simply swept aside. Within a matter of weeks, the RAF was driven back to Burma and India.

ROMMEL

On 21 January 1942, the Germans once more went on the offensive in the Western Desert. The Allies fell back in some disarray, their WDAF air cover bogged down on flooded airstrips. The problem was temporary and as Rommel consolidated his gains and tried to resupply, the WDAF went on the attack once more, blitzing crucial supply lines and using ground controllers to call in close air support strikes for troops. At the same time, the WDAF proved itself a formidable force in the air, claiming over 600 *'kills'* in just three months.

LEFT: RAF recruitment poster

RIGHT: Colourised image, Cologne Cathedral stands seemingly undamaged (although having been directly hit several times and damaged severely) while entire area surrounding it is completely devastated

THE AVRO LANCASTER

'...the best night bomber of the war...'
Adolf Galland

The four engine Avro Lancaster evolved out of the disappointing twin engine Avro Manchester and went on to become the RAF's main heavy night bomber of the war. Sir Arthur Harris, Head of Bomber Command, called it his *'shining sword.'* The Lancaster first entered service in January 1942 with first 44 and then 90 Squadron.

Its long, unobstructed bomb bay had been fortuitously designed, which meant it could carry virtually any type of bomb the RAF needed it to carry, including 4000lb (the Cookie or *'Dangerous Dustbin'*), 8000lb, 12,000 lb Blockbusters and Tallboys and 22,000lb Grand Slams (A bomb so heavy it weighed the same as the Lancaster itself). It could even carry the unique *'Bouncing Bombs'* designed by Barnes Wallis and used by 617 Squadron on the famous *'Dam Busters'* raid of 1943. In total the Lancaster dropped 608,612 long tons of bombs during the war over 156,000 sorties.

7,377 Lancasters were built of which 3,249 were shot down, and nine of the 32 VCs awarded to RAF air crew went to Lancaster pilots and crew.

MAIN IMAGE: Lancaster B Mk1s of No. 50 Squadron, Royal Air Force, based at Skellingthorpe, flying in spread formation. The two aircraft beyond the wing tip are `VN-D' and `VN-J' the former, serial number JA899, was missing on the night of 24 - 25 June 1944 with Pilot Officer L G Peters and crew

FAR LEFT: Line drawing of Lancaster B Mk1

ABOVE CLOCKWISE FROM TOP LEFT: Avro Lancaster bombers nearing completion at the A V Roe & Co Ltd factory, Woodford, Cheshire; The rear gunner of a Lancaster of No. 44 Squadron peeks out through a cut-out in the perspex of his gun turret, October 1942; Mechanics work on the port engines of an Avro Lancaster of No 207 Squadron, near the technical site at Bottesford; Armourers make final checks on the bomb load of an Avro Lancaster B Mark I of No. 207 Squadron RAF at Syerston, Nottinghamshire, before a night bombing operation to Bremen

REAPING THE WHIRLWIND

In late February 1942, Air Marshal Sir Arthur Harris became C-in-C of RAF Bomber Command. He brought with him a radical new direction for the service. From now on, under Harris's command, the RAF's bombing campaign would be to directly target *'the morale of the enemy civil population and in particular of the industrial workers'*. Rather than going after highly specific targets — still a daunting task — they would now rely on Area Bombing. The Germans, he said, *'have sown the wind, and they shall reap the whirlwind'*. Harris's arrival also coincided with a powerful new navigation aid, *'Gee',* to help bombers find

BELOW: RAF Air Chief Marshal Sir Arthur Harris

RIGHT: The flour mill at Rangoon after having been destroyed by an RAF. 500 pound bomb

their targets. Gee — a combination of three triangulating navigation beams — was first tried out on a raid on the Renault Factory near Paris in March 1942. The results were spectacular. More than 220 bombers delivered their loads directly on target. Two further raids confirmed Harris's faith in the system and he set his bomber force — which was enjoying a simultaneous increase in heavy bomber deliveries — against the Ruhr.

On 30/31 May 1942, the RAF launched its first-ever 1,000 bomber raid on Cologne — 'Operation Millennium'. It was easily four times the size of any previous RAF bomber raid and was put together by scrounging up resources from just about wherever they could be found. It was all finished inside an hour and a half. Over 910 bombers actually hit the target, cascading down incendiaries and high explosives. As the bombers returned to their bases the conflagration they had left behind could be seen from 150 miles away. Forty two RAF bombers were lost.

BURMA AND INDIA

In January 1942, the RAF and Flying Tiger contingents still holding out in Rangoon, Burma, received reinforcements — 30 Hurricanes and 113 Squadron flying Blenheims. Incredibly, the local RAF commander, D.F. Stevenson, decided to go on the offensive with what he had and the Blenheims managed to surprise and destroy 58 Japanese aircraft on the ground. As Allied troops battled to retreat towards India, the RAF contingent fought on for three months against overwhelming odds to buy precious time. They were all but wiped out by 22 March.

With Burma lost, the RAF spent 1942 desperately trying to build up their strength in India, but few aircraft could be spared for the Far Eastern theatre and typically they would only receive almost obsolete aircraft such as the Blenheim, Wellington and Hurricane.

1942 was also the year in which the new 'Burma Road' was established, with 31 and 194 Squadron Dakotas joining USAAF transports in flying essential war supplies to the beleaguered Chinese to keep them in the war against Japan. At the height of operations, Allied transports would take off into some of the most treacherous flying conditions on earth *'over the hump'* — the imposing Patkai Mountains — to China. Allied transports would also play a vital role in resupplying British

Chindit raiders — commandos roaming the jungles behind enemy lines in search of tempting targets — the following year.

THE RAF REGIMENT

The Blitzkrieg of 1940 showed the need for the RAF to have its own ground troops to defend its airfields. The RAF Regiment was established by Royal Warrant in January 1942. Shortly after, it developed two different types of Squadrons — one responsible for manning anti-aircraft guns and the second armed with mortars, anti-tank guns and armoured cars responsible for tackling enemy ground forces. By D-Day 1944, the regiment consisted of 240 Squadrons and 85,000 serving officers and men deployed in every theatre.

Post war, the RAF Regiment took an active role in protect vulnerable RAF bases in the last wars of Empire and today is playing an active role in both the Iraq/Syria and Afghanistan conflicts.

COASTAL COMMAND – CHANGING FORTUNES

Just as the Battle of the Atlantic seemed hopeless, Britain's fortunes abruptly changed. After the Enigma Code was cracked at Bletchley Park, submarine positions in the Atlantic became almost an open book. At the same time, both the battleships Gneisenau and Lutzow were badly damaged after being torpedoed by Beauforts, and the Bismarck sunk by the Royal Navy.

With the US entering the war, U-boat Wulf Packs started to prowl the east coast of America in early 1942, before moving more to the centre of the Atlantic, where they hoped Coastal Command and American maritime units couldn't reach them. Coastal Command's response was to employ aircraft with longer

LEFT TOP: An RAF Regiment crew mans a 40 mm Bofors anti-aircraft gun near an advanced landing ground in Normandy, France

LEFT BOTTOM: Men of the RAF Regiment practising techniques in getting over a high wall during training on an assault course at Bradwell Bay, Essex

RIGHT: RAF Air Chief Marshal Sir Arthur Tedder

ranges such as the Halifax and American B-17 Flying Fortress to strike them, which they did with increasing effectiveness. The tide had not yet turned in the Allies favour though. The convoys were still losing half a million tons of shipping per month in the second half of 1942 culminating in a loss of 814,700 tons in November 1942 — the worst single loss suffered in the entire war.

THE PATHFINDERS

In 1942, the Pathfinder Group was formed. Comprised of some of Bomber Command's finest crews and flying a combination of Lancasters and the impressive new Mosquito, the Pathfinders were designed to fly ahead of the main bomber force and drop flares and incendiary bombs to mark the target. Despite early German successes in jamming *'Gee'*, Pathfinders did this successfully on about 75% of missions. Before it could be proved completely successful as a tactic, RAF Bomber Command's attention was switched temporarily to industrial targets in Northern Italy to support the ground war then raging in the Mediterranean.

THE DESERT AIR FORCE DAF

In January 1943, Air Chief Marshal Tedder, the Middle East Air Force commander, assumed command of all Allied air forces in North Africa and the Mediterranean, and air power played a vital role in ending the last Axis resistance on the African continent by destroying their ability to reinforce and resupply by air. In just three weeks, Allied air power accounted for 432 enemy transports for the loss of just 35 fighters. Vital lessons such as the proper co-ordination of army and air force were subsequently applied to the Italian Campaign and the Invasion of Europe to outstanding effect.

BOMBER COMMAND IN 1943

By March 1943, Harris could call upon 62 bomber squadrons — 36 of which were *'heavy'*. That month he launched what became known as *'The Battle of the Ruhr'*, blitzing Essen — the home of the Krupps works — three

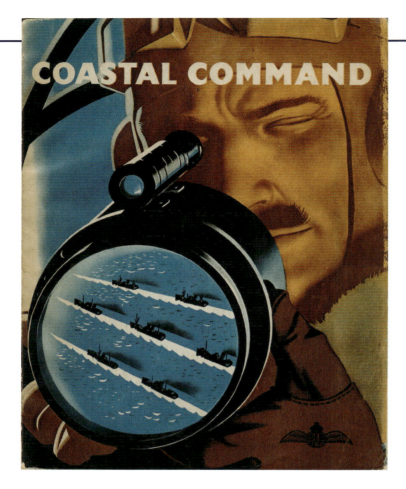

COASTAL COMMAND

the target, almost completely blinding the local radar and thereof anti-aircraft gun co-ordination and night fighter instructions. Hamburg was devastated in a series of RAF and USAAF strikes between July and August. Over 60% of the homes in the city were destroyed and over 42,000 killed by blast and firestorm. Refugees streamed out, depriving the surviving factories of their work force and manufacturing in the city was brought to a standstill for many weeks.

Raids on Berlin in late 1943 and early 1944 were not as successful, mainly because of atrocious weather conditions and swarms of German night fighters armed with onboard radar and devastating *'Jazz Music'* cannon. 123 RAF bombers were lost on the first three major raids alone, the majority shot down by Luftwaffe night fighters. From November 1943 to March 1944, the RAF lost a total of 492 bombers over the German capital.

RAF TRANSPORT COMMAND

RAF Transport Command was formed on 25 March 1943, taking over its responsibilities from RAF Ferry Command and becoming the logistics arm of the RAF. Later, it would assume responsibility for dropping paratroops from Army Cooperation Command, and did so famously during both D-Day and Arnhem. It was Transport Command's job to supply Allied forces in every theatre of the war, flying everything from the Dakota to converted Liberators.

U-BOAT HUNTING.

In January 1943, at the Casablanca Conference, it was agreed that one of the most pressing war aims was to eliminate the U-boat menace. While Coastal Command now had better planes, armaments and detection equipment, it was still a very formidable task. In May 1943, Coastal Command succeeded in sinking no fewer than 19 submarines out of a total of 41 destroyed that month. After that the Wulf Packs decided to largely abandon the northern Atlantic and concentrated on what they considered to be safer waters around the Bay of

times, as well as striking Duisburg and Dusseldorf and targets further afield. During the first half of the year, Bomber Command conducted 43 raids against targets in the Ruhr. One of these was the world-famous *'Dambusters'* raid, which saw Lancasters of 617 Squadron attack the Mohne and Eder dams with special *'bouncing bombs'*. The raid caused havoc to water and power supplies in the region. 1943 also saw the introduction of a number of new navigational aids for the bombers, including H2S and OBOE (later to be refined and renamed as GH).

The first American B-17 and B-24 bombers had started flying raids from England in the late summer of 1942. By 1943, Germany was being struck around the clock, with USAAF (the US Army Air Force) bombers striking by day and RAF Bomber Command launching raids by night. Fighter Command provided Spitfire escorts for the American bombers to supplement USAAF's own Mustangs and Thunderbolts.

In July, Bomber Command turned its attention to Hamburg. Here it used a new weapon. *'Window'* was a tactic of dropping showers of aluminium foil over

TOP LEFT: Front cover of Coastal Command, 1943. Coastal Command was a booklet issued for the Air Ministry by the Ministry of Information

RIGHT: Aerial photo showing the bombing of a German U-boat or submarine base in Pola, Italy during World War II

Biscay. Coastal Command accordingly packed the area with search aircraft, including newly adapted Sunderlands with nose turret guns. By the end of 1943, Coastal Command had sunk a total of 90 U-boats and damaged a further 51.

PREPARING FOR D-DAY

The planned Allied invasion of France, scheduled now for the summer of 1944, could not happen if the RAF and USAAF could not achieve total aerial superiority over the landing beaches. With that in mind, the RAF embarked on an ambitious programme of restructuring. No2 Group of Bomber Command — basically all their light and medium day bombers — were given over to Fighter Command in June 1943. Fighter Command itself was temporarily ended in November 1943 (to return in October 1944), now splitting into the 2nd Tactical Air Force (for use in Europe) and the Air Defence of Great Britain (which would comprise 10 day and 11 night fighter squadrons). The 2nd Tactical became part of the joint Allied Expeditionary Air Force, commanded by Air Marshal Trafford Leigh-Mallory.

D-DAY

In preparation for D-Day, the Allied Expeditionary Air Force pounded France with the intention of destroying the nation's transport infrastructure. Lancasters and Halifaxes hit railway junctions and marshalling yards by night, while USAAF bombers pounded the same targets by day. The raids caused major damage to France's railway network for minimal losses. Attention then switched to radar stations, roads and bridges in the Normandy region and German-occupied airfields before finally concentrating on the coastal defences themselves.

As the invasion fleet came in on the morning of 6 June 1944, RAF Lancasters and Stirlings dropped 'Window' to knock out German radar and continued to hit coastal batteries. In excess of 5,000 tons of bombs rained down on just ten German coastal batteries alone. The fleet was protected by the greatest assembly of air power ever seen — 9,120 Allied warplanes including 2,000 RAF fighters. The Luftwaffe simply couldn't rise to the challenge and only two enemy aircraft were seen over the beaches on D-Day. As troops pressed inland off the beaches, Bomber Command

supported them with large scale raids to dislodge stubborn German resistance. In the months that followed, Bomber Command repeatedly flew against the besieged ports still held by the Germans, and succeeded in dislodging them from Calais, Le Havre and Boulogne. They flew too in close support, blitzing German lines just a couple of miles from the advancing Allies. At the same time, RAF Typhoons, Tempests and Spitfires launched devastating ground attacks with machine guns, cannons and rockets on any German concentrations of men, supplies and armour.

RETAKING BURMA

At the start of 1944, SEAC was intensifying its fight against the Japanese in Burma, launching withering ground attacks on enemy supply lines and successfully preventing significant Japanese reinforcements from reaching the front. Incredibly, the Japanese chose this moment to launch their invasion of India — straight into a gauntlet of Allied Aerial firepower such as they had never experienced before. Allied troops were able to hold, enjoying close air support with Allied forward ground controllers calling up the next available aircraft in the 'taxi rank' above to hit the target. The tactics pioneered by the RAF in North Africa were now paying dividends thousands of miles away. Meanwhile, reliable aerial resupply missions kept the Allied troops sufficient in provisions and ammunition.

By June, their attack blunted, the Japanese army started a fighting retreat. As they fell back they were pounded by Hurricane fighter-bomber variants as well as new American-made Liberator bombers and Thunderbolts, both now being flown by RAF Squadrons. As the Allied troops advanced, they

RIGHT: The Air Chiefs for the allied invasion, March 1944. Back row standing L-R: Col E. C. Langmead, Air Vice Marshal J. B. Cole-Hamilton, Major General W. O. Butler, Air Chief Marshal Sir Trafford Leigh-Mallory, Major General H. S. Vandenberg, Air Vice Marshal H. E. P. Wigglesworth, Air Vice marshal C. H. K. Edmonds, Major General Ralph Royce. Front row seated L-R: Air Vice Marshal L. N. Hollingshurst, Air Marshal Sir Arthur Coningham, Major General L. H. Brereton, Air Vice Marshal H. W. L. Saunders, Air Marshal Sir Roderick M. Hill

were kept well supplied and supported by the seventeen squadrons of the British and American Combat Cargo Task Force. In the skies, the Japanese presence withered to just 125 planes by the end of the year.

GERMANY UNDER PRESSURE

In 1944, despite the massed bombing raids, Germany managed to increase the productivity of its factories. This did not mean that the effort had been a waste. German morale was collapsing. Far from the glorious early days of the Reich, now the German people faced almost certain destruction and ignoble defeat. Resources that were badly needed on the eastern and western fronts had to be instead given to defence of Germany's cities and what was left of the Luftwaffe was tied up in defence of the Reich itself, rather than supporting German troops in their desperate battles elsewhere.

In the skies above enemy territory, RAF night raids increased in ferocity. In the last three months of 1944, as Luftwaffe resistance began to fragment and then crumble, Bomber Command dropped 163,000 tons of bombs (In the same three months of 1942, the total had been just 8,000 tons). When the RAF went after Dursburg, in just 24 hours they dropped more bombs on the city than had been dropped on London during the whole war. In December alone, over 15,000 bombers struck the Reich — and the Germans only managed to bring down 135 of them.

The destructive power of the strategic bomber offensive unleashed against Germany in the final year of the war was astounding — and unsurvivable.

MAIN IMAGE: A Consolidated Liberator Mark II of No. 159 Squadron RAF is refuelled at Salbani, India, before undertaking a raid on the docks at Rangoon, Burma

ABOVE: Aerial shot of devastated Dresden

Dresden was hit by 773 aircraft of Bomber Command on the nights of 13 and 14 February 1945, with USAAF hitting the same city by day on the 14th and 15th. The casualty figure — including those listed as *'missing'* (ie incinerated or else blown to pieces) topped 54,000. On 6 April 1945, the policy of Area Bombing finally came to an end. It had done its job.

BURMA AND THE FAR EAST

By early 1945, Japanese control over Burma was crumbling. Such was the power of the Allied bomber fleet that it could now strike targets up to 3,000 miles from its bases. It could hit small strategic targets with radio-controlled bombs, or simply *'carpet bomb'* an area where the Japanese were known to be massing. Ground attack aircraft such as RAF Thunderbolts had a new and fearsome weapon at their disposal — napalm. Rangoon fell back in Allied hands on 2 May 1945. On 6 and 9 August, American B-29 Super-Fortresses dropped atomic bombs on Hiroshima and Nagasaki — and the war was done.

A HARD-WON FIGHT

At the start of the Second World War, despite a desperate race to re-arm, the RAF had faced the enemy with first rate pilots, aircrew and ground crews — but also with largely third rate (and too few) aircraft and poor technology and armaments — a legacy of decades of financial starvation. While the fighters

were up to the job of Home Defence, the quality of British bombers took years to improve sufficiently for the bomber force to make any real impact. It was the contribution behind the scenes of British ingenuity and technical and scientific prowess which finally put the first rate men into first rate machines and gave them the aids and the armaments they needed to do the job.

70,253 RAF personnel died in the war: 47,293 of those were from Bomber Command. Bomber Command was to suffer some of the highest casualty rates of the entire war. In just one raid (on Nuremburg in March 1944), they lost more men than Fighter Command did during the entire Battle of Britain. A further 4,000 men died serving with Fighter Command. Bomber Command flew 364,514 during hostilities. By the end of the war, Coastal Command had flown 240,000 sorties for the loss of 1,777 aircraft and 5,866 men. They had sunk 213 U-boats, damaged a further 120 and accounted for 366 German ships.

CASTLE TO COTTAGE

By the end of the Second World War, the Royal Air Force comprised over 9,000 aircraft and almost 1,200,000 men and women. Only the 42 squadrons of RAF Transport Command were in any real demand, to move personnel around, run supplies into parts of the world left devastated by the war and to repatriate prisoners. Bombers were hastily converted into makeshift transports, with luggage stored in their bomb bays.

As might have been expected, the move to dismantle the wartime RAF

began with a degree of haste and no little amount of confusion. Many squadrons were entirely disbanded and their aircraft simply sent to the scrapyards. Aircraft production lines were abruptly switched off and never restarted. Demobilisation led to the RAF losing almost 900,000 personnel within just two years and Fighter command was reduced to strength of just 200 aircraft. Whitehall wasn't too sure what a post-war RAF would look like — but whatever form it took, it would be considerably cheaper.

INTO THE JET AGE

The first post-war jet fighter squadrons began to appear in 1946. First three, then six RAF squadrons were equipped with the Meteor F3. New twin tail boom de Havilland Vampires joined 247 Squadron that same year and the first all-Vampire Wing comprising three Squadrons was in place by September 1946.

MAIN IMAGE: Ground crew refuelling a Gloster Meteor F Mk III of No. 616 Squadron RAF at Manston, Kent, 4 January 1945

OPP. PAGE LEFT: A Royal Air Force Hunting Percival Provost T.1 (WV429) flies alongside De Havilland Vampire T.11 (XD520), both possibly from No. 5 Flying Training School, at RAF Oakington, Cambridgeshire

OPP. PAGE RIGHT: Four Royal Air Force De Havilland Vampire FB.9s in line abreast formation over Egyptian desert

There was no real jet equivalent for Bomber Command, and the Lancaster continued to be the backbone of the service while its new variant, the Avro Lincoln, had been slowly replacing it since the late autumn of 1945. RAF Transport Command made do with another Lancaster variant, the Avro York, as well as a full assortment of spare wartime types including *'cleaned up'* ex-bombers.

THE BOMB

As the Government hurriedly tried to make sense of what would be needed of a post-war RAF, one of the key questions was whether or not Britain would develop its own nuclear bomb. By 1947, the decision had been taken — Britain would have its own nuclear deterrent — and the RAF would have custody of it.

That same year, the Air Staff finally decided what the post-war RAF would look like in its *'Plan E',* based on the assumption that the Soviet Union was most likely to be the new enemy. The phrase *'Cold War'* had just been used for the first time. The RAF would comprise fifty one fighter and forty one bomber squadrons, forty two transport squadrons and thirteen maritime squadrons, with a further reserve of 12 squadrons. The newly shaped service would possess some 1250 aircraft in all.

THE NEW THREAT

In June 1948, Russia decided to test the West's resolve by blocking all rail and road transport links into Berlin, which was set deep with Soviet-controlled East Germany. In response, the Allies decided to use the three available air corridors to supply the city from the skies. Alongside the Americans, the RAF began to fly an intensive air supply operation that would eventually bring in up to 5,000 short tons of food and other essentials every single day to meet the desperate needs of two million trapped Berliners. At its height, a relief transport was landing in the city once every three minutes. The Berlin Airlift, as it is remembered today, worked and the Soviets ended their land blockade of the German capital in May 1949 with no little loss of face.

BANDING TOGETHER

The Blockade of Berlin was a wakeup call — if one were needed — that the Soviets were a growing threat. Belgium, the Netherlands, Luxembourg, France, and the United Kingdom had already entered into a mutual defence treaty against the Soviets in 1947 and other events including the Communist seizure of Czechoslovakia and the blockade of Berlin would lead to the formation of NATO (The North Atlantic Treaty Organisation) in April 1949. The original group formed by the five European powers were joined by Canada, Denmark, Iceland, Italy, Norway, Portugal and the United States. More would join later.

OPERATION FIREDOG · MALAYA

International Communism was not just a direct threat in Europe. It also fed and inspired numerous anti-Empire movements across the globe as a new political reality began to take shape. The Communist rebellion in Malaya was not an uprising by the indigenous Malay people, but a terrorist movement among Chinese immigrants. With much of the country made up of thick jungle, air power was essential to attack enemy camps and supply routes and to move troops around. On 16 June 1948, a month after an *'Emergency'* was declared, Spitfires of 28 and 60 Squadrons arrived in Kuala Lumpur to provide air support. They were soon joined by Beaufighters, Dakotas and Sunderlands. Austers and Single and Twin Pioneers flew reconnaissance missions, while Dakotas and Valetta's dropped supplies to troops in the jungle. Helicopters came to play a significant part too, with the first casualty evacuation unit established in 1950 flying Dragonflies. Few guessed that the RAF would be fighting there for twelve years, with 31 different aircraft types taking part.

BELOW LEFT: A civil registered Avro Tudor C5, G-AKBZ 'Star Falcon', at Wunstorf aerodrome during the Berlin Airlift, 1948. This aircraft was used as a fuel freighter during the Airlift

BELOW RIGHT: A Short Sunderland GR Mark 5 of No 201 Squadron, Royal Air Force, moored on the Havel in Berlin

RIGHT: RAF gunner in a Sunderland bomber in Malaya

FROM COTTAGE TO CASTLE AGAIN

The need to build an effective Cold War RAF to meet the Soviet threat led to a significant and swift expansion. In 1950, the RAF had 4,500 aircraft. By 1952, that number had risen to 6,338, with 277,000 personnel. As the decade went on, the Lancasters of Coastal Command were replaced by the Shackleton and Transport Command received its first jets, as Comets joined 216 Squadron in 1956.

RAF Fighter Command had been ambitiously dismantled by 1949. Now it grew again. By 1952, its numbers had more than doubled, while the Royal Auxiliary Air Force provided another 160 aircraft if required. It was temporarily equipped with American F-86 Sabre jets until the British aircraft industry could catch up. By 1954, Britain had two new exceptional home grown fighters in the Supermarine Swift and the Hawker Hunter. While the Swift did not live up to early expectations and had to be relegated to a low level fighter-reconnaissance role, the Hunter would progress to become the RAF's main frontline fighter aircraft until the 1960s. Two years later, the Hunter was joined by the Javelin, the first RAF aircraft to carry air-to-air missiles as standard. By 1956, RAF Fighter Command could boast thirty five squadrons and 600 aircraft.

The post war RAF presence in Europe had been initially slashed to just ten squadrons by 1947. Now, Europe was the frontline in any war against the Soviets. At the start of 1952, the RAF had sixteen squadrons in theatre, mainly comprising Meteors and Vampires, which were now serving as part of NATO as part of the new 2nd Allied Tactical Air Force (2ATAF). As the RAF strength in 2ATAF grew to twenty-five squadrons, the Vampires were phased out in favour of new Venom fighter-bombers and American Sabres pressed into service. As time passed, new Hawker Hunters replaced the Sabres. Four squadrons of Canberras also joined the force *'on loan'* from Bomber Command.

In 1949, Bomber Command had barely 150 aircraft to its name and was temporarily reinforced with old American B-29s, renamed Washingtons.

By 1950, however, it was starting to be equipped with a truly world-beating British bomber - the English Electric Canberra. Offering excellent performance and speeds of over 500 mph, Canberras would serve as frontline bombers until the 1960s. The Canberra for all its virtues could not deliver a nuclear weapon and Bomber Command would have to wait until mid-decade for the arrival of aircraft capable of delivering Britain's Blue Danube free fall atomic bomb.

V-FORCE

It took Britain almost eight years to build its own bombers capable of launching a nuclear strike, from an initial Ministry of Supply Specification in 1947. The first V-bomber, the Vickers Valiant, arrived in 1955. The next V-Bomber, the Avro Vulcan, entered service in 1956. The third V-Bomber, the Handley Page Victor, appeared the following year.

Together the three V-Bombers stationed on ten especially enlarged RAF bases would comprise V-Force, which would carry nuclear bombloads behind the Iron Curtain if called upon. Britain now had its nuclear deterrent in place and the philosophy of MAD (Mutually Assured Destruction) ruled strategic thinking.

RIGHT: An RAF pilot wearing a high altitude helmet. 43 Squadron were the first to be equipped with jet fighters

THE AVRO VULCAN

The delta wing Vulcan bomber was first delivered to RAF Bomber Command in 1956 and the first Vulcan Squadron, No 83, was formed in May 1957.

The Vulcan had no defensive weapons on board, relying on its high altitude and electronic countermeasures to be able to run any gauntlet of enemy interceptors and SAMs. The B1 model quickly gave way to the B2, with better Electronic Countermeasure defences and a longer range. It would also be able to carry Blue Steel — a nuclear missile which could be fired off 100 miles from target. Despite these changes, there was still concern that Vulcans would be unable to penetrate the ever-improving Soviet air defences and from 1966 onwards plans switched drastically from a high level strike to low level attacks.

MAIN IMAGE: AVRO Vulcan bomber in flight

RIGHT: Line diagram of Avro Vulcan B Mk 2

OPP. PAGE CLOCKWISE FROM TOP RIGHT: Vulcan Bomb bay; Rolls-Royce Bristol Siddeley Olympus Mk.301 jet engine; Vulcan bombers from RAF Waddington flying in formation in 1957; Cockpit of an Avro Vulcan B2

SUEZ

In 1956, growing tension between an increasingly eastern-leaning Egypt and Britain and France flared into open conflict when Egypt seized control of the strategically vital Suez Canal. War broke out between the Israelis and Egyptians almost simultaneously. An ultimatum to both sides by Britain and France was accepted by the Israelis but refused by Egypt. On the evening of 31 October, RAF Canberras flew from Malta to strike twelve Egyptian air bases close to the canal. Two more nights of bombing followed, with daylight raids carried out by RAF fighters and components of the Fleet Air Arm, who had five aircraft carriers on station. In the first week, over 250 Egyptian aircraft were destroyed, with no RAF losses. On November 5, RAF Hastings and Valettas dropped British paratroopers around Port Said. A hasty ceasefire was convened the same day, as the British and French governments caved in to aggressive American disapproval and Soviet threats of nuclear war if Egypt fell.

SANDYS

It is often said that Suez marked the end of Britain as a world power. This humiliating experience, coupled with the still-crippling financial legacy of fighting World War Two, changed British political priorities forever. British Prime Minister Harold Macmillan may have told the nation, *'You've never had it so good'* — but at the same time he was desperately casting around for huge spending cuts — and the armed forces looked very tempting. As Chancellor, Macmillan had told Anthony Eden *'It is defence (spending) that has broken our backs. We also know that we get no defence from (it)'*.

In 1957, Minister of Defence Duncan Sandys produced a Defence White Paper after being told by Macmillan to find £100 million worth of savings in his department. The old adage of *'The Bomber will always get through'* had returned with a modern twist. In the age of the H-bomb, conventional

RIGHT: Britain's 'V-Bomber trio' - the 'Vulcan', 'Valiant',and 'Victor' - are seen in this air-to-air picture flying in formation over Southern England, in the course of development flying from the Ministry of Supply's Establishment at Boscombe Down

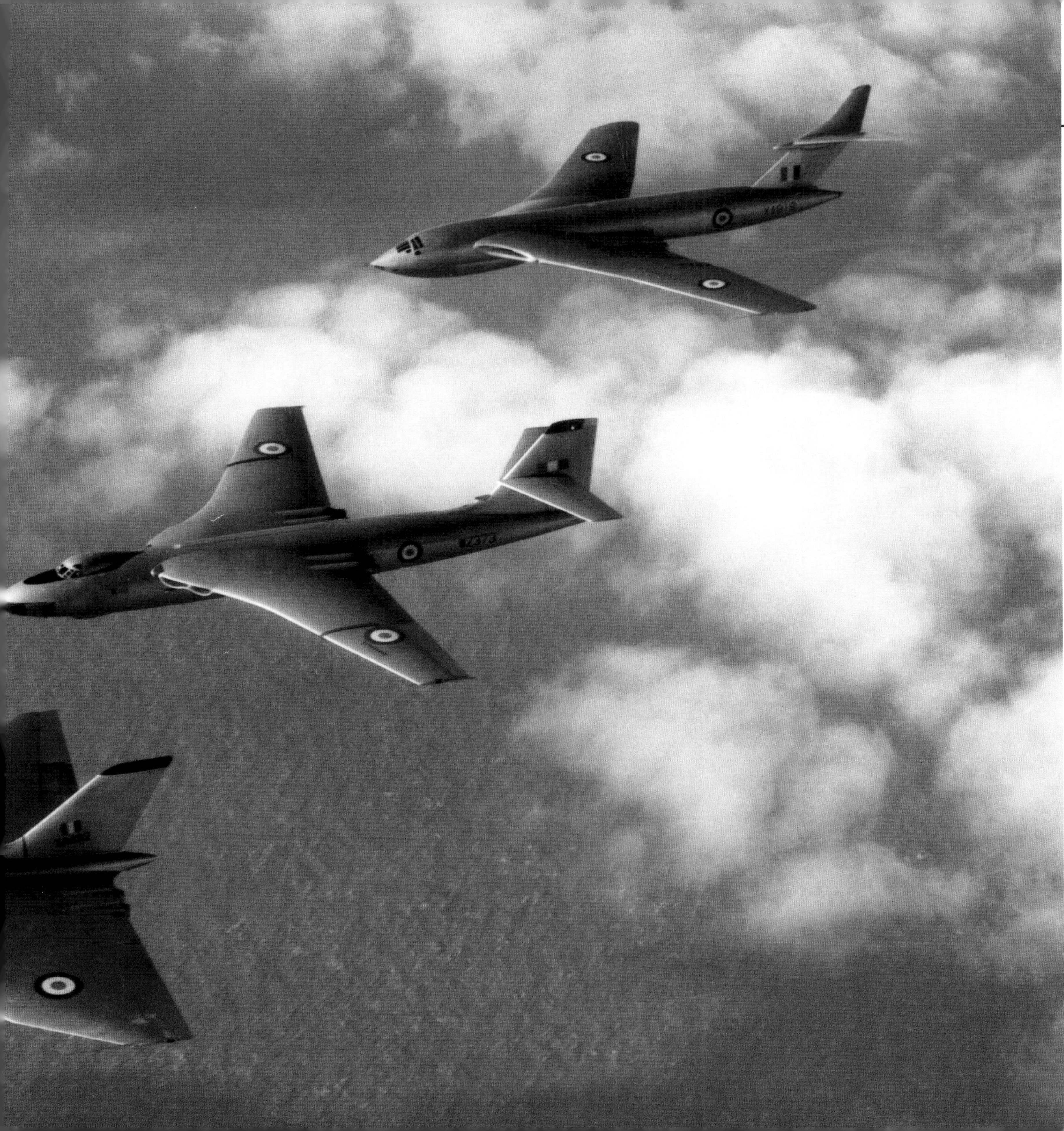

forces seemed almost irrelevant. Now, *'the Missile would always get through'* — and all the nation really needed was its nuclear deterrent. This would be delivered by V-Bombers in the short term, until inevitably replaced with missiles. Fighter aircraft were now irrelevant, except to protect the V-Bomber bases. Even the 2ATAF NATO commitment could be cut, with RAF squadrons in Europe slashed to just eighteen.

Accordingly, virtually every new British aircraft project was cancelled, except for the Lightning (too far along) and what would be the TSR-2 (a tactical nuclear delivery system). The Avro 720, the Hawker Siddeley P.1121, the Fairey Delta 2, and the Saunders-Roe SR.177 were all lost. At first Fighter Command itself was scheduled to be closed down, but was then reprieved, albeit scaled back to just an airfield defence role with far fewer planes. British aircraft designers were *'encouraged'* with some vigour to merge together to

form the British Aircraft Corporation. This would signal the end of Britain as a significant player in world aviation design.

MISSILES

It was now officially the Age of the Missile. Bloodhound surface to air missiles started to appear on RAF V-bomber bases. In 1958, the first Mach 15 Douglas Thor intermediate range nuclear missiles were installed on RAF air fields around Britain and were operated by 20 RAF squadrons. Thors were American, but Britain was dutifully trying to develop a medium range ballistic missile of its own, codenamed *'Blue Streak'*. The project was initially believed to cost £50 million. By the start of the 1960s, cost estimates for Blue Streak had risen to £1.3 billion and the project was abandoned.

THE BATTLE OF BRITAIN MEMORIAL FLIGHT

The Battle of Britain Memorial Flight (BoBMF) was established by the RAF in 1957, *'to maintain the priceless artefacts of our national heritage in airworthy condition in order to commemorate those who have fallen in the service of this country, to promote the modern day Air Force and to inspire the future generations'*.

Still a highlight at any British air display today over fifty years later, the present BoBMF is based at RAF Coningsby and currently comprises six Spitfires, two Hurricane Mk 2Cs, a Lancaster, a C47 Dakota and two Chipmunk aircraft (for training purposes).

RIGHT: Engineers inside high pressure vessel, Bristol Siddeley Aircraft, 1959 testing the Mk320 Olympus engine designed for the TSR-2 jet aircraft which was abandoned by the government after only a few flights

ABOVE: Battle Of Britain Memorial Flight in 2012

WARS OF EMPIRE

The Malayan *'Emergency'* officially came to an end in July 1960. As part of Operation Firedog, RAF aircraft had flown 375,849 sorties. However, plenty more *'wars of empire'* were flaring up to vex a Britain convinced that conventional warfare was over and all a country needed in the way of defence was The Bomb. The Mau-Mau rebellion in Kenya, which had begun in 1952 was still continuing into 1960, despite the use of everything from converted RAF trainers to Avro Lincolns to bomb them. There was trouble in Thailand and Oman, and Cypriots were demanding unity with either Greece or Turkey, depending on their religion. Britain would need to take a role in the dispute between Indonesia and Malaysia in North Borneo. Kuwait needed to be protected from its bellicose neighbour Iraq after gaining independence. In 1963, the British Crown Colony of Aden (now Southern Yemen) saw a surge in Arab nationalism. Tensions simmered until 1967, by which time the RAF were using squadrons of Hunters stationed at RAF Khormaksar, Aden, to strafe rebel bases with rockets and 30mm cannon. None of these *'little wars'* could be ended by nuclear weapons. It was clear that there was a flaw in Duncan Sandys' thinking.

EMERGENCY FLIGHTS

Missiles were equally unsuited to replacing RAF aircraft as they assumed a growing humanitarian role. Operation *'Tana Flood'* in October 1961 saw RAF Transport Command assigned to delivering humanitarian supplies to parts of Kenya cut off by floods. The operation was then extended to deliver four months' worth of humanitarian supplies to Somaliland. The Command was stretched by simultaneously needing to fly in relief supplies to British Honduras after a devastating Hurricane.

BELOW LEFT: RAF Avro Lincoln cockpit

BELOW RIGHT: Avro Lincolns lined up

RIGHT: Aerial view of missile site in Cuba

FAR RIGHT: John F Kennedy

THE CUBAN MISSILE CRISIS

On 16 October 1962, a U-2 spyplane overflew over Communist Cuba and spotted nuclear missile sites being prepared on the island, just 100 miles off the coast of America. The Cold War heated up in a matter of days and a jittery game of brinkmanship played out, reaching a peak on 26 October with a transatlantic phone call between Kennedy and Prime Minister Macmillan. Kennedy still hadn't made a decision, and Soviet ships were already steaming towards Cuba laden with nuclear missiles.

In Britain, forty aircraft of V-Force were *'bombed up'* with nuclear weapons and put on the highest state of readiness, ready to take off in minutes if the word to *'Scramble'* came. Bomber crews even took to wearing their Mae West life jackets and catching what sleep they could in caravans next to their aircraft. At one point, they were so sure that the *'Scramble'* call would come that crews sat inside their aircraft with engines running. Tensions were finally scaled back when Soviet leader Khrushchev agreed to remove the missiles from Cuba if the US would remove their Thor nuclear missiles from Turkey.

THE ENGLISH ELECTRIC / BAC LIGHTNING

The Lightning was the first — and last — all-British Mach 2 fighter. Originally conceived to defend V-Bomber bases with short-range, high speed attacks on enemy bomber formations, it was soon given a wider QRA role in intercepting any intruders coming close to British air space. With its phenomenal rate of climb, pilots would liken it to being *'saddled to a sky rocket'*.

The Lightning had its origins in a 1947 specification and development work continued right up until the end of the 1950s. The first Lightning F1s finally entered service with RAF Fighter Command 74 Squadron at Coltishall in July 1960. Pilots found them easy to fly but early models were a struggle to maintain. A small number of variants were developed, culminating in the F.6. New tanks were added to increase range and the choice of weaponry became more powerful. Higher thrust engines and bombing capability were also introduced.

The British government only ever saw the Lightning as a stop gap until interceptors could be fully replaced by missiles, perhaps by 1970, and so actively held back development and discouraged exports. By the time they had realised that fighters were far from obsolete, the Lightning had fallen behind other aircraft capabilities. There were now no British designs on the drawing board and it had to be replaced by an aircraft built in America — the F4 Phantom — for air defence. Despite this, a limited number of Lightnings continued to serve with the RAF until as late as 1988. 337 Lightnings were built in all.

MAIN IMAGE: English Electric Lightning F3 at RAF Lakenheath

BELOW LEFT: Line drawing of Lightning F3

OPP. PAGE L-R: English Electric Lightning landing at Filton, Bristol, England; Nine Lightning F.1 of No.74 Squadron RAF display at the 1961 SBAC show, Farnborough; Lightnings of No 56 Squadron during Armament Practice Camp at Akrotiri, In the foreground, a technician is preparing a Firestreak missile for loading

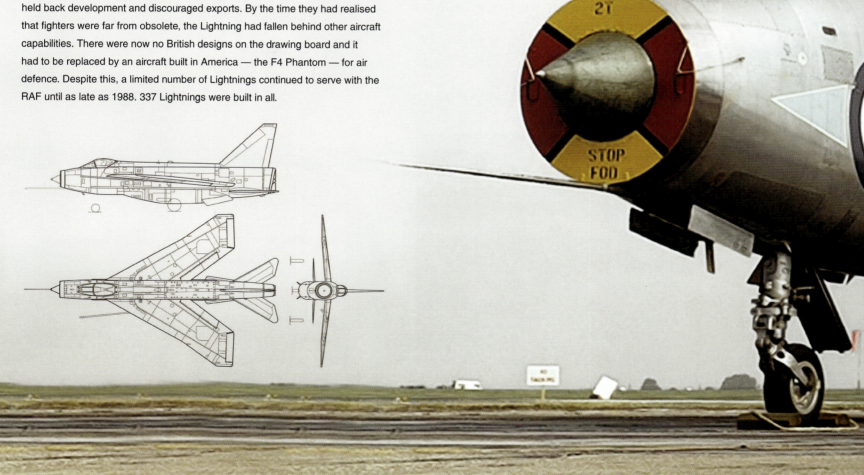

THE FALL OF THE MISSILES

Whether the government wanted to hear it or not, missiles are increasingly looking like an unlikely replacement for warplanes. Most Bloodhound SAMs were removed from RAF airfields by 1964. The Thor missiles, it was determined, would take at least 15 minutes to launch — and that meant they were useless in a world with a new *'four minute warning'*. They were all unceremoniously returned to America in 1963. Britain's own medium range missile, Blue Streak, proved impossibly expensive and was duly cancelled in favour of the American Skybolt, which was then cancelled by the Americans in short order leaving Britain with nothing except the V-Force's aircraft-launched Blue Steel missile or free fall bombs. In the end, the Americans agreed to sell Britain Polaris A3 missiles at a quite exceptionally low price. These would be installed in Resolution-class submarines. The Royal Navy then assumed official control of Britain's nuclear deterrent from the RAF in 1968.

ADDICTED TO CUTS

While the argument in favour of relying on missiles was already starting to fall apart, the prospect of achieving real cost savings by slashing the armed forces was a temptation neither Conservative nor Labour governments could resist.

By 1962, RAF squadrons in West Germany had already been reduced to just twelve and in 1965, Fighter Command could only count on flying a meagre sixty aircraft. In July 1952, the RAF had a strength of 6,338 aircraft. By 1967, the force had been *'slenderised'* (a government term) to just 2,004. By 1973, it would be *'slenderised'* further to just over 500 aircraft. Even the V-Force started to be dismantled between 1967-9 as part of the preparations for Polaris, from a June 1964 peak with 50 Valiants, 70 Vulcans and 39 Victors in service.

Gibraltar would lose its only operational squadron by 1966, as part of a series of determined closures of air stations abroad. A year later it was announced that the RAF would be withdrawn from both the Far and Middle East by no later than the end of 1971.

In 1965, fresh government cuts delivered a series of body blows to the RAF. Firstly, the government announced the cancellation of the P.1154 V/STOL supersonic interceptor and the HS 681 V/STOL transports. Britain would buy American Phantoms and C-130 transports instead. Then just three months later, they scrapped the potentially world-beating British BAC TSR-2 program for good measure.

THE TSR-2

'All modern aircraft have four dimensions: span, length, height and politics. TSR-2 simply got the first three right'

Sir Sydney Camm, designer of the Hawker Hurricane

Intended as a replacement for the RAF's aging Canberras, the TSR-2 was intended as an ultra-low level, high speed nuclear strike and reconnaissance aircraft. It would be, by almost universal agreement, the finest, most advanced aircraft of its type anywhere in the world. However, the project was cancelled on

cost grounds in 1965 by Chancellor Denis Healy. Such was the vitriol against the TSR-2 in some quarters of the Labour Party (who saw the TSR-2 as a Conservative elitist *'prestige project'*) that the only airframe ever to fly, XR219, (along with two partially completed aircraft) were used for target practice and destroyed. Other airframes were scrapped in front of cameras or vandalised. Not only were the aircraft destroyed, but all film and still photography of the TSR-2 was ordered to be burned. Even a wooden mock-up was torched.

Instead the government elected to buy American swing wing F-111 Aardvarks to do the job on the grounds that they would be cheaper. They turned out to be more expensive, so expensive in fact that the government then cancelled an order for 50 Aardvarks in January 1968, incurring a huge cancellation penalty. Eventually, Phantoms and Blackburn Buccaneers (particularly hated in the higher ranks of the RAF) would fill the gap, despite both aircraft types having been evaluated and rejected years ago in favour of the TSR-2. Phantoms would serve with the RAF until 1992.

ALL CHANGE AT THE TOP

In 1964, the British government established the Ministry for Defence. Instead of having its own dedicated Air Ministry, the RAF would now be regulated through the Air Force Department of the Ministry of Defence.

In April 1968, Fighter Command merged with Bomber Command to form Strike Command. Just over a year later, Coastal Command would also be merged into Strike Command. Cost savings were achieved.

THE SANDYS ERROR

By the late 1960s, the full error of the Sandys White Paper was obviously apparent. Manned warplanes were still very much needed for the foreseeable future — but next to nothing was being developed and the British aviation industry was in ruins. The RAF would now be required as quickly as possible to reassume most of its previous responsibilities. There was just one catch — the government weren't going to pay for it.

ABOVE LEFT: A Canberra aircraft flying high

ABOVE RIGHT: British bomber TSR2 in flight

OPP. PAGE: Thor missiles were stored horizontally in covered shelters, and elevated to a vertical position for fuelling just before launch

RAF AEROBATIC DISPLAY TEAMS

The world famous RAF Red Arrows display team was set up in 1964. The team made their debut appearance flying seven Gnat trainers at the 1965 Biggin Hill Air Fair. Three years later they increased their numbers to nine, making the 'Diamond Nine' formation their signature display, and converted to BAE Hawk trainers in 1980. Today, they are globally respected as one of the world's greatest display teams and have made almost 5,000 appearances around the globe. Their motto is simply eclat, meaning 'excellence'.

The RAF display team is a long and cherished tradition, dating back to the formation aerobatics performed at the earliest Hendon Air Pageants with Sopwith Snipes initially stealing the show. After the Second World War, squadrons formed their own unofficial display teams and a somewhat bewildering number of different display teams were present at public events. In the early 1950s, there were several different Vampire and Meteor teams. By the mid-1950s, Hawker Hunters were the aircraft of choice.
In 1956, the black-painted Hawker Hunters of 111 Squadron were selected as the RAF's official aerobatic display team. The 'Black Arrows' as they became known, regularly performed with as many as sixteen jets at the height of their popularity and set a new world record by looping no less than twenty-two Hunters over crowds at Farnborough in 1958.

In 1961, 92 Squadron 'Blue Diamond' Hunters replaced the Black Arrows, before they too were replaced by the Tigers and then the Firebirds. Both teams flew English Electric Lightnings but — in an era when military costs were not appreciated — the sheer expense of a flying display performed by frontline fighters proved unappealing. They were stopped in favour of the Red Pelicans flying six Jet Provost trainers and the Yellowjacks flying five yellow Gnat trainers. Since it was more economical to fly one team than two, they were then replaced in short order by the Red Arrows, who have officially represented the RAF ever since.

MAIN IMAGE: Spectators watch a display from the Red Arrows (Royal Air Force Aerobatic Team), 27th April 1967

ABOVE RIGHT: Line drawing of Hawker Hunter

OPP. PAGE: The Red Arrows of today do their thing

THE HAWKER SIDDELEY HARRIER

The Harrier 'Jump Jet' somehow survived the many cuts and cancellations of the 1960s, mainly because Hawker Siddeley had such faith in its unique vertical take-off and landing design that it took no government money for its development.

It came into service with the RAF at the very end of the 1960s, and it was recognised as just perfect for service in Germany. Most NATO air bases were expected to be obliterated in a thermonuclear blast, but the Harrier's unique VTOL capabilities meant that it could be dispersed and then fight back from virtually anywhere — a forest clearing, a car park, an empty field or a town square. It could, offer close air support to NATO troops or strike Warsaw Pact armoured columns.

The Harrier was never intended to dogfight, but proved a lethal opponent in battles with Argentinian aircraft during the Falklands War. It also saw action in Iraq, the Balkans and Afghanistan. Government cuts finally caught up with it in 2010 when it was announced that the Harrier was being prematurely retired. Eighty three planes were sold off to the US Marine Corps.

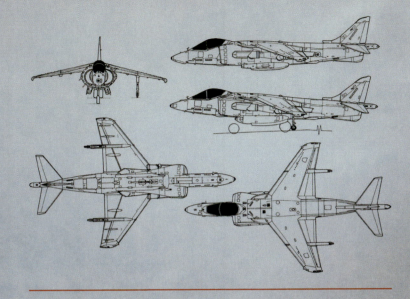

MAIN IMAGE: A Harrier GR9 from IV Squadron, RAF Cottesmore is pictured during a sortie over Afghanistan. Paveway IV laser guided bombs can be seen on the outermost pylon underneath the wings

ABOVE: Line Drawing of Harrier

OPP. PAGE L–R: British Aerospace Harrier GR5; Harrier hidden in Belize 1979; A Joint Force Harrier jet is pictured high over RAF Akrotiri in Cyprus shortly before the iconic aircraft was decommissioned

THE CUTTING EDGE

As the 1970s began, the RAF was in a situation that was depressingly familiar. The calibre of its pilots, aircrew and ground staff was uniformly excellent, but in the main it was flying aircraft that were almost obsolete — and there was nothing that could be done about it for years to come. The RAF still had Shackletons, Lightnings and Canberras — as well as seven squadrons of ex-nuclear deterrent Vulcans it hardly knew what to do with.

Not only were the warplanes being flown largely out of date, but there were undeniably fewer of them too. In 1967, the RAF could put up 2004 aircraft. By 1973, that total had dropped to just over 600 — and further cuts were to follow. Three squadrons of Comets and Britannia transports were disbanded during 1975. The following year, half of the remaining RAF communications squadrons were scrapped, to be followed at the start of 1977 by cuts in the RAF tanker force amounting to a full third. The thinking was that Britain only needed to deliver troops and supplies to NATO in West Germany and to the worsening situation in Northern Ireland. The days of long range missions and policing the far reaches of Empire were long gone. After all, by October 1971, the RAF had no squadrons left in the Far East.

More reorganisations began, supposedly for 'efficiency' but no doubt with cost-cutting in mind. In 1972, Air Support Command was rolled up into Strike Command. A year later, Maintenance Command was restructured and renamed Support Command.

NATO IN EUROPE

Despite the seemingly never ending cuts and restructuring exercises, in the early 1970s the RAF was ordered to increase its commitment to NATO in Europe. By the end of the decade, a full quarter of its strength was to be found overseas in West Germany. The first squadron of Harriers arrived in Germany in June 1970 and the first Phantom FGR2s in August. Further Harrier and Phantom squadrons were to follow, along with Jaguars and Buccaneers.

THE JAGUAR

In May 1973, the first two SEPECAT Jaguar GR1 fighter-bombers arrived at No. 226 OCU at Lossiemouth. An Anglo-French project, the Jaguar had escaped cancellation during development because it was intended as a badly-needed replacement for old (and therefore expensive) RAF trainers. It was only later that it was considered as a warplane — by an RAF desperate to have something at least semi-modern to fly and fight with. It was discovered too that the aircraft could even deliver a tactical nuclear bomb. This happy accident continued to serve successfully with the RAF until 2007, being phased out in favour of the Tornado and Typhoon.

MORE HOPE ON THE HORIZON

In 1975-6, Britain, Italy and Germany agreed to buy 809 Panavia Tornado MRCA's. The Tornado it was generally agreed, would finally give the RAF the capabilities it would have had over a decade earlier had the TSR-2 seen service.

Towards the end of the decade, moves were made to do whatever could be done to strengthen the RAF. While the Tornado would not be ready, Hawker trainers could be introduced to replace Gnats and Hunters in that role. Old Search and Rescue Whirlwind and Wessex helicopters started to be replaced by Sikorsky Sea Kings, and RAF helicopter transport squadrons were promised new American Chinooks. The RAF's airborne refuelling capacity — which had now been allowed to dwindle down to just two Victor K2 Squadrons - was promised nine new Super VC10s to form a third squadron. On Maritime duties, 1940s era Shackletons started to be replaced with the Hawker Siddeley Nimrod, which itself was an adapted 1950s Comet airliner, but at least it was a jet.

OPP. PAGE CLOCKWISE FROM TOP LEFT: McDonnell Douglas F-4K Phantom; SEPECAT Jaguar; Panavia Tornado; Hawker Siddeley Buccaneer

A CLEAR IMBALANCE

At the end of the decade, on paper at least the RAF had expanded and could now claim something like 1,800 aircraft at best. Of those, only 400 could fight. Phantoms were still defending British skies, and the aging Buccaneer was the primary long range fighter. By comparison, the Soviet Air Force could rely on receiving churning out 1800 warplanes every single year, and were investing heavily in new aviation technology...

THE TORNADO ARRIVES

In June 1981, the first PANAVIA Tornados were supplied to RAF Honington for training purposes. With the Tornados on their way, the remaining Vulcan squadrons began to be disbanded with vigour. 617 (the famous Dambusters Squadron) went on 31 December 1981, with the intent of likewise disbanding all the remaining Vulcan squadrons in the first six months of 1982. Two more squadrons of Tornados became operational in 1983 and Tornados were despatched to West Germany for the first time, but British air defences were still heavily reliant on elderly Phantoms and Lightnings.

OPERATION CORPORATE – THE FALKLANDS WAR

Just as the RAF was being ordered to dismantle its long range capabilities, so a war broke out somewhat inconveniently 8000 miles away.

The fascist junta in control of Argentina, in a desperate attempt to distract the people from its ineptitude and brutality, invaded the Falkland Islands in the far South Atlantic. Britain decided to fight back. On 5 April 1982, a naval

task force left Portsmouth bound for the Islands. The campaign would largely depend on the Army, the Royal Navy and the Fleet Air Arm. RAF Nimrods flew protective cover as the Task Force sailed.

The RAF responded just a day after the invasion, as eight Hercules transports flew to Ascension Island and the American air base there known as 'Wideawake'. 3,900 miles from the Falklands — and about the same distance from Britain - it provided the only realistic air base for supply and support operations. In the days that followed, Wideawake saw a massive increase in activity as more RAF planes poured in, including anti-submarine Nimrods. Victor tankers for long range refuelling arrived on 18 and 19 April. They had been rush modified with special radar and photo reconnaissance equipment to give them multi role capabilities in theatre. The first Vulcan bombers arrived on 29 April. Again the aircraft received significant technical changes before they flew out, while their crews were given an intensive refresher course in conventional bombing techniques. No one had really anticipated using Vulcans in a conventional bombing role and such skills had long atrophied.

On 30 April, the two Vulcan bombers flew out of Ascension to bomb Port Stanley Airfield on the first 'Black Buck' missions, to deny its use to Argentine planes. One Vulcan had to turn back with mechanical problems, but the other met no defensive fire as, just before dawn, it swept over the airfield and dropped 21 1000lb bombs. One hit the centre line of the runway. Others destroyed parked Argentinian warplanes and buildings. The attack was then followed up first by a Sea Harrier strike and then a bombardment from the guns of naval warships offshore. The Vulcans returned on 4 May to deliver more bombs on the airfield. The 'Black Buck' missions were the longest bomber missions ever undertaken in any conflict since the dawn of aviation. The skilled RAF crews flew round trips of almost 8,500 miles taking just under sixteen hours with each plane burning 22,000 gallons of fuel. They required air to air refuelling from a fleet of eleven Victor tankers no less than seven times on the outward flight — and once on their return. To pull off the operation, even the tankers themselves required air-to-air refuelling. It was an incredible achievement.

While three Squadrons of Fleet Air Arm Harriers sailed with the task force, the first RAF Harriers (from 1 Squadron) flew non-stop out to Ascension on 3 May, with more to follow. They then embarked for operations off the carriers HMS Hermes and Invincible, primarily in a ground support role. They blitzed enemy fuel dumps close to Fox Bay on 20 May, but lost an aircraft the following day from ground fire as the Harriers flew close support for the British troops landing at San Carlos Bay. Two more RAF Harriers were lost to ground fire but none to enemy aircraft. Seven RAF pilots also flew a number of FAA Sea Harriers and scored a number of *'Kills'*.

Vulcans returned to action in early June, now fitted with Shrike missiles and targeted against enemy radar posts, while RAF Victors and Nimrods flew photoreconnaissance missions, Nimrods flew search and rescue and Hercules transports dropped supplies to British troops as they advanced,. One last Vulcan mission was flown on 11 June. On 15 June, the Argentineans surrendered.

According to MOD figures, the air war cost the Argentinians 117 aircraft confirmed destroyed or listed as *'probables'*. On the British side, ten Harriers was lost, a full half of them to accidents. Twenty three helicopters were also lost, all on board ships hit by enemy fire. No British pilots died. It was an

OPP. PAGE: Vulcan bomber making an approach to land at Ascension Island during Falklands War, 1982

BELOW: Royal Navy sailors of the destroyer HMS Sheffield, attacked and eventually sunk by Argentinian forces during the Falklands War, arrive back home on a RAF VC10 aircraft at RAF Brize Norton in Oxfordshire on 27th May 1982

incredible military feat and a resounding victory, against a background of budget cuts that had forced all the armed services included the RAF to fight at the very limits of their resources and capabilities.

Determined not to be caught out again by Argentinian aggression, work began almost immediately to build a permanent air base on the Islands. Sea Harriers shielded the islands until F-4 Phantoms flew in to provide air protection. They were replaced by Tornado F3s. Since 2007, the islands have been guarded by Typhoons.

RECOVERING THE RANGE

The Falklands War served as an abrupt awakening, not least as a challenge to the wisdom of running down Britain's air-to-air refuelling capabilities. Yet another about-face was performed and suddenly the 50 Squadron Vulcans scheduled to be scrapped were hastily converted into tankers, as were a number of Hercules transports. They helped to fill a vital gap until Lockheed Tristar 500s and VC10 K2s became available in mid-1983.

THE END OF AN ERA

In March 1985, Mikhail Gorbachev was appointed leader of the Soviet Union. With him came new policies. Russia intended to be more open and transparent with greater freedom of speech and free elections. Gorbachev also wanted to see an end to the ruinously expensive Arms Race that the Soviet Union had been locked into since the 1940s. The Eastern Bloc could not survive the sweeping changes that it unwittingly unleashed. By 1989, Eastern European countries were tearing themselves free of the Warsaw Pact and struggling to become democracies. On 9 November, the Berlin Wall separating east and west was torn down by jubilant crowds. The Soviet Union itself officially ceased to exist on Boxing Day 1991, the Communist flag having been lowered over the Kremlin on 25 December. The Cold War was finally over. Now, what was to be done with a Cold war sized RAF?

RIGHT: A Royal Air Force VC10

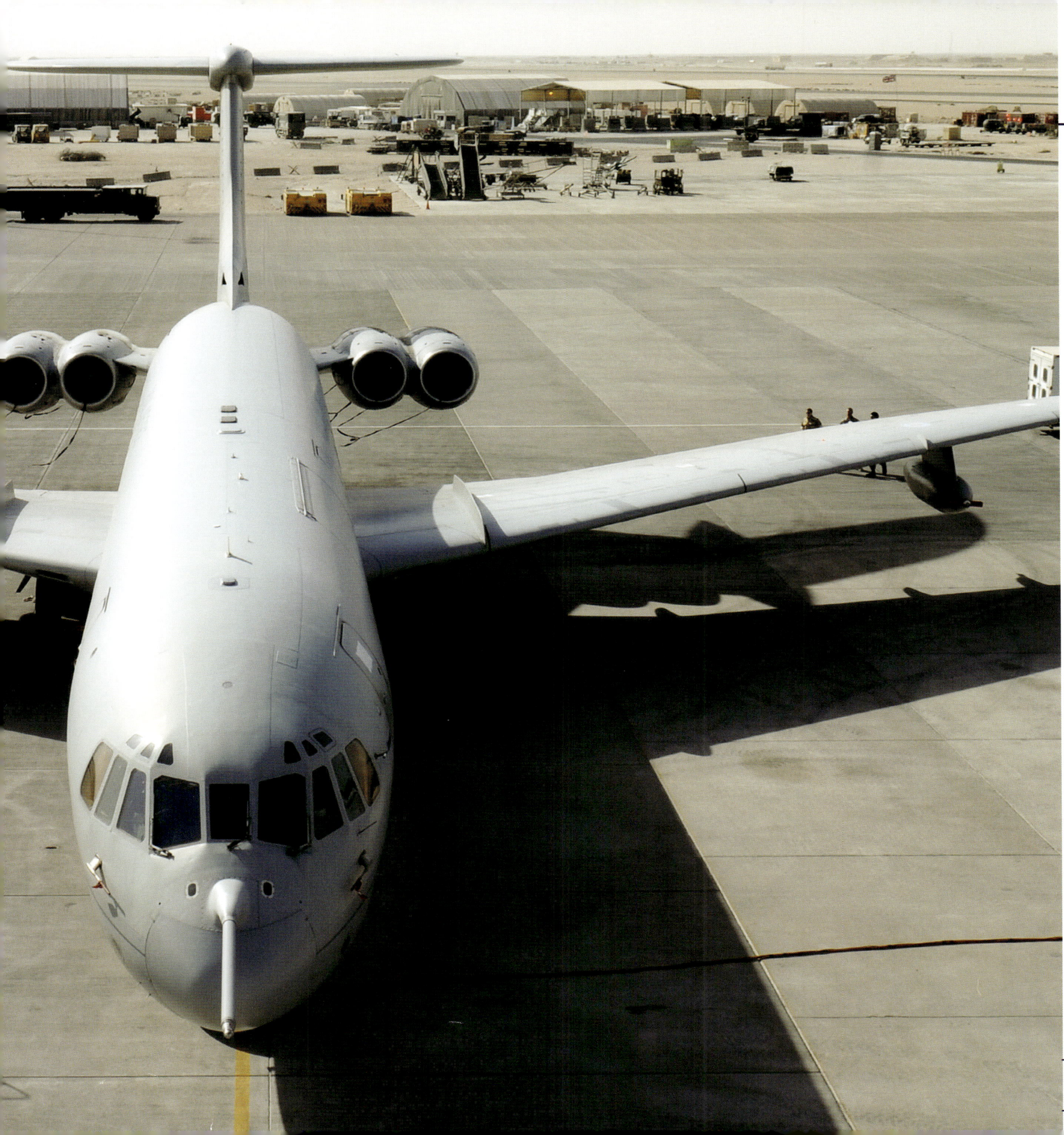

THE PANAVIA TORNADO

The RAF call it *'The Tonka'*. Developed by British Aerospace in a consortium with German and Italian partners, the Tornado was designed as three variants to fill three different roles. The IDS was designed as a fighter bomber (designated by the RAF as the GR1 and then the GR4 upgrade), the ADV as an interceptor (F2-3) and the ECR for electronic countermeasure warfare and reconnaissance.

Introduced into RAF squadron service in 1982, it first saw action in the 1991 Gulf War where over 50 Tornados were flown. RAF Tornados would also fight in the Balkans War of the 1990s, during the Second Iraq War, the Afghanistan Conflict and over Libya, and are now being used against ISIS in Iraq and Syria.

After the Millennium, potential cost savings of £7.5 billion led to support for a move to scrap the entire RAF Tornado fleet, but the Strategic Defence and Security Review in 2010 decided to dispense with the Harrier instead. Tornados will however be gradually phased out in favour of the Typhoon and then the F-35.

MAIN IMAGE: A Tornado GR4 from 125 Squadron based at RAF Lossiemouth soars high above the clouds over the UK

BELOW LEFT: Line drawing of Panavia Tornado

OPP. PAGE CLOCKWISE FROM TOP LEFT: German air force GR-4 Tornado refuels using a drogue-and-hose system from a U.S. Air Force KC-10 Extender near Mosul, Iraq; Vickers VC-10 in aerial refuelling exercise with Tornados; Royal Air Force VC10, in the tanker role, carries out the air-to-air refuelling of a two RAF Tornado F3s; An RAF Tornado GR4 aircraft carrying two Storm Shadow missiles under the fuselage

A NEW WAR

The rapid collapse of the Soviet Union and the Warsaw Pact both surprised and confused NATO. Almost no-one had foreseen it. The Cold War was over and the assembled air forces stationed in Europe suddenly had no-one to face off against. Politicians began to look for a peace dividend which would inevitably mean deep service cuts.

WAR IN THE DESERT – OPERATION GRANBY

In August 1990, Iraq invaded Kuwait. There were also serious concerns that its rogue leader, Saddam Hussein, would go on to threaten Saudi Arabia. Within just 48 hours of the British government confirming its commitment to freeing the small Gulf state and providing a deterrent to further Iraqi aggression, Tornado F-3 interceptors were sent to bases in Saudi Arabia and Oman. Two days later, they were joined by a squadron of Jaguar fighter-bombers and then VC10 tankers and Nimrod maritime patrol aircraft.

Within a further two days, another squadron of Jaguar fighters-bombers arrived, together with half a squadron of VC10 tanker aircraft and soon after they were joined by half a squadron of Nimrod maritime patrol aircraft. By mid-January 1991, the full contingent standing by in the desert also included further Tornados, Chinook and Puma helicopters, seven Hercules transports and elements of the RAF Regiment.

The destruction of the Iraqi Air Force was judged the first priority. On the night of 16/17 January 1991, RAF Tornado GR1s began low level attacks on giant Iraqi Airfields, dropping JP233 anti-runway munitions, 1,000lb bombs and ALARM radar suppression missiles.. Their missions were supported by VC10 K2/3 and Victor K2 tanker aircraft. USAF F-15s flew Combat Air Patrols to protect the GR1s as they flew in at low level, while F-4G Wild Weasels' hit SAM sites and EF-111A 'Raven' electronic countermeasures aircraft disrupted enemy radar. Despite this, four GR-3s were lost to enemy ground fire over four days and nights, and low level attacks on airfields were abandoned in favour of higher level strikes.

The Tornado GR1s were joined by Jaguars and quickly widened their role to destroying vehicles, barracks and storage areas. On 19 January, Jaguars began to hunt SAM sites and artillery emplacements. By the night of 21/22 January, the Tornados had also expanded their role to take out SCUD missile sites, ammunition dumps and radar installations, while the Jaguars proved particularly effective against Iraqi shipping.

By 2 February, RAF Buccaneers were available to provide laser designation of ground targets and Tornados went into action to disrupt Iraqi supply lines

LEFT: A Royal Air Force SEPECAT Jaguar GR1 aircraft (s/n XZ355) from No. 41 Squadron, RAF, takes off during operation Desert Shield on 23 January 1991

RIGHT: British and U.S. Air Force ground crew members refuel a Royal Air Force SEPECAT Jaguar GR1 aircraft from No. 41 Squadron, RAF, during Operation Desert Shield on 23 January 1991

between Iraq and Kuwait, blitzing thirty bridges over the Tigris and Euphrates. When the bridge infrastructure was sufficiently degraded, the RAF went after the Southern Iraqi airfields, delivering a knockout blow to Saddam's hopes of his air force denying the liberation of Kuwait. In turn, the Jaguars switched to hitting SAM and AA sites hastily assembled by the invading military.
All RAF offensive sorties ceased at 03.00 hours GMT on 28 February — but crews were held on two hours readiness. All objectives were considered met and vast columns of Iraqi troops were fleeing Kuwait.

Almost 2,500 sorties were flown by RAF Tornados during the Gulf War, along with 200 Buccaneer and 600 Jaguar sorties. Six Tornados were lost in action. A seventh was downed by an engine fire. A Jaguar was also lost. Behind the scenes, RAF transports had already exceeded the achievements of the massive Berlin Airlift in terms of tonnage even before the shooting started. They also brought 26,000 personnel into Saudi and Oman. RAF Puma and Chinook helicopters flew over 700 sorties doing everything from resupply runs to Special Forces insertions.

Although most aircraft flew home after the conflict, the RAF helped USAF in maintaining a *'No Fly Zone'* operation over Iraq from 1991 to 2003, during which time many strikes would continue to be made against Iraqi radar and anti-aircraft sites.

MISSIONS OF MERCY

The RAF continued to prove itself in an enlarged humanitarian role. In May 1991, RAF Hercules and Chinook transports delivered vital supplies to the Kurds seeking shelter from Saddam's regime, while the following year the RAF flew out Gurkha engineers to help Western Samoa after it was hit by a cyclone. The RAF also delivered famine relief to Somalia and essential supplies to the city of Sarajevo which was caught in the fast-developing Balkans War. Relief flights to Sarajevo would continue until 1996.

DRAWDOWN FROM GERMANY

Under the *'Options for Change'* programme of reductions, RAF Wildenrath in Germany became the first station to cease all fixed wing flying in April 1992. 60 Squadron was disbanded. RAF Gutersloh in Germany closed a year later after having been home to the RAF for forty eight years. A month after the closure of Gutersloh, RAF Germany itself was officially ended. On 1 Apr 1996, 2 Group at Rheindahlen disbanded and with them went the final RAF HQ on continental Europe. The last remaining RAF base in Germany — RAF Brüggen — closed in 2001.

Further afield, the last RAF contingent in Belize withdrew its Puma helicopters in 1994. Two years later the last RAF base in mainland Asia, Sek Kong, closed down. 28 Squadron relocated its Wessex HC2 helicopters to Kai Tak commercial airport in Hong Kong, awaiting the handover to the Chinese in 1997.

RIGHT: RAF Hercules C130 Delivers Stores

WOMEN IN THE ROYAL AIR FORCE

On the day the Royal Air Force was established in 1918, the Women's Royal Air Force (WRAF) also came in to being. The women were largely inherited from the RFC and RNAS where they had been working mostly as clerks, typists, cooks and maids. There would also be opportunities for driving and pigeon keeping. The daughters of the well-to-do automatically came in at officer level. In 1920, the WRAF was scrapped and 32,000 women were dismissed with haste.

It was only when another World War threatened that women were brought back. Since 1938, women had served in 48 RAF companies as part of the Auxiliary Territorial Service. This became the Women's Auxiliary Air Force (WAAF) on 28 June 1939. At the height of the war, there were almost 200,000 WAAFs. They could not participate as aircrew (the women who flew ferry missions were civilians), but could now work as intelligence and photo analysis specialists, radar operatives, aircraft mechanics and codebreakers as well as in more mundane clerical and catering roles.

At the end of the Second World War, most were demobbed and when the WAAF returned to its original name of the Women's RAF on 1 February 1949, the organisation was just a few hundred strong. The distinctions between the RAF and the WRAF were gradually whittled away as more roles became open to women, and the RAF and WRAF were formally merged in 1994.

In 1990, Flight Lieutenant Julie Gibson officially became RAF's first operational female pilot and in 1992 the RAF announced that women would in future be allowed to fly Fast Jets. The first operational Fast Jet pilot was Flight Lieutenant Jo Salter, initially flying a Tornado GR1B with the celebrated 617 *'Dam Busters'* Squadron. Since then, women pilots have flown combat operations over Afghanistan and Iraq, as well as QRA in defence of Britain. In 2007, helicopter pilot Flight Lieutenant Michelle Goodman won the Distinguished Flying Cross (DFC) for her heroism in rescuing casualties under fire in Basra and in 2010, Flight Lieutenant Kirsty Moore became the first woman ever to fly with the prestigious Red Arrows display team. With the decision in 2017 to allow women in the RAF Regiment to take part in close combat, there is now no role in the Royal Air Force that is still closed to women.

MAIN IMAGE: The first woman pilot to join the Red Arrows, Flight Lieutenant Kirsty Moore, stands by her Hawk aircraft at RAF Scampton in Lincoln, northern England on November 12, 2009

BELOW CLOCKWISE FROM LEFT: A fitter of the WAAF working on the Liberty engine of a De Havilland 9A; WAAF and ATS recruitment poster; A WAAF signals officer tests the intercom system in an Avro Lancaster, WWII; WAAF and RAF trainee ground crew work together on a Hawker Hart as part of Commonwealth Joint Air Training at Waterkloof near Pretoria, South Africa

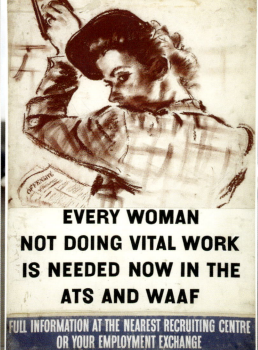

EVERY WOMAN NOT DOING VITAL WORK IS NEEDED NOW IN THE ATS AND WAAF

FULL INFORMATION AT THE NEAREST RECRUITING CENTRE OR YOUR EMPLOYMENT EXCHANGE

OPERATION DESERT FOX

Operation Desert Fox in December 1998 saw RAF Tornados joining USAF F-117s in the skies over Iraq as the West lost patience with Saddam's non-compliance and interference with inspectors searching for caches of Weapons of Mass Destruction. Over 4 days and nights from 16 to 19 December, USAF and the RAF joined forces in a punitive series of strikes. Over 600 sorties were flown by more than 300 combat and support aircraft. Twelve Tornado GR1s from 12 Squadron, already on station in Kuwait, took part with support from VC10 Tankers and Hercules. In total the Tornados flew 32 medium level sorties during Desert Fox and dropped 61 Paveway 2 and Paveway 3 LGBs. Among their targets was the facility housing Saddam's infamous L29 *'Drones of Death'*, remotely piloted vehicles capable of delivering both chemical and biological weapons.

WAR IN THE BALKANS

As the former Yugoslavia fell apart after the death of its former dictator, Tito, ethnic and religious tensions dating back hundreds of years finally flared up into a sporadic war that spanned the 1990s. As early as 1993, RAF Tornado F3s and AWACS aircraft contributed to Operation Deny Flight, NATO's operation to restrict airspace movements over Bosnia and Herzegovina.

The operation continued until late 1995. NATO aircraft (including the RAF) became ever more involved in hostile operations against the Serbs. Strikes reached a Crescendo in 1999 after the Serbs invaded Kosovo and began a program of genocide against Albanian Muslims. Operation Allied Force wiped out all military targets within three days, and then continued to degrade the infrastructure of Serbia between March and June. 1,000 aircraft took part, and the RAF strike contribution consisted mostly of Harriers that were later joined by Tornados. Serbia effectively surrendered after 3 June.

THE 1998 STRATEGIC DEFENCE REVIEW

In the summer of 1998, the Strategic Defence Review proposed a number of important changes for the RAF. The Review, by a now Labour government, was partly in response to lessons learned during the Gulf War and operations in the Balkans. They included early retirement for its VC10 and Tristar tankers (The Hercules tanker fleet had already disbanded in 1996) — to be replaced with an as yet undecided type. Given global volatility, it was also suggested that four American C-17 Globemaster III transports be purchased for the Rapid Reaction Force. The Royal Navy's two squadrons of Sea Harriers were to merge with the RAF's four squadrons of GR7s, becoming Joint Force Harrier. The helicopter forces of all three services would pool together as *'Joint Helicopter Command'*.

MAIN IMAGE: A Harrier GR9 from IV Squadron, RAF Cottesmore prior to a sortie over Afghanistan. Paveway IV laser guided bombs can be seen on the outermost pylons underneath the wings

9/11

Just as it seemed that the world would see some years of peace, Islamist terrorists belonging to Al Qaeda attacked the New York's World Trade Centre and the Pentagon in Washington DC by flying hijacked airliners into them. A fourth suicide attack was foiled over Pennsylvania when heroic passengers on United Airlines Flight 93 turned on their hijackers and forced the plane down. 2,996 people died in the attack — the worst act of terrorism ever seen on American soil.

AFGHANISTAN

The USA responded by attacking Afghanistan. Although the vast majority of Hijackers were Saudis, the Islamist Taliban regime in Afghanistan had given shelter to the Al Qaeda high command and its leader, Osama Bin Laden. British forces went with them.

In October 2001, the RAF began Operation Veritas (later Operation Herrick) against the Taliban in Afghanistan, with Tristar and VC10 tankers deployed to refuel both British and US Navy aircraft. Transports included the C-130 Hercules and Chinook and Merlin Helicopters. In 2004, they were joined by six Joint Force Harrier GR7s from No. 3 Squadron, deployed to Afghanistan to provide close air support and reconnaissance for ISAF and Coalition forces. More Harriers would follow until they were withdrawn from Afghanistan in 2009 in favour of Tornado GR4s. Sentinel and Reaper Drones were also deployed in 2007. Between 2006 and 2010, Harriers and Tornados flew approximately 160 sorties per month.

RAF and Army helicopters flew some of the most perilous missions of the war, often coming under small arms or RPG fire while landing troops or supplies in remote areas. The threat was so serious that pilots were instructed to stay on the ground for no more than 30 seconds. Their vital role in the Afghan campaign was acknowledged by the government in 2009, when they announced the intent to purchase 22 new Chinooks for the RAF, principally for use in Afghanistan.

HOME DEFENCE

Since 9/11, RAF fighters have been kept on QRA to deal with terrorist incidents, most probably the hijacking of a civilian aircraft. During the London 2012 Olympics, the threat of terrorist attack was judged so grave that the

QRA Typhoons were augmented with Sentry airborne warning radar aircraft and fighter aircraft were moved to RAF Northolt in Greater London itself.

In 2007, the Typhoon officially took on the QRA role in protecting British airspace. While the Typhoon upgraded its ground attack abilities, Tornados were used to fill in the gap left by the Jaguar.

THE SECOND GULF WAR

In March 2003, the Second Gulf War broke out as the UN declared Iraq in breach of a number of its resolutions.

The invasion of Iraq raged from 20 March to 1 May, during which time the RAF flew 2,519 sorties, 1,353 of which were offensive strikes. The British part in the Coalition fight was named Operation Telic. After the fall of Baghdad and the execution of Saddam, Merlin, Puma and Chinook helicopters continued to operate out of Basra in the South of the country as part of 903 Expeditionary Air Wing with RAF Regiment protection. Insurgency was rife in Basra though, and in 2005, nine airmen and a soldier were killed when an RAF Hercules was shot down by insurgents. Basra was abandoned in 2007 and all RAF operations in Iraq officially ceased in 2009.

THE TYPHOON TAKES CHARGE

The Typhoon multi-role fighter began RAF service in 2006 with 3 Squadron and Jaguars were retired after over 30 years of service the following year.

OPP. PAGE LEFT: A Lockheed Tristar K.1 (s/n ZD951) of No. 216 Squadron, Royal Air Force, refuels U.S. Navy McDonnell Douglas F/A-18C Hornet fighters

OPP. PAGE RIGHT: Royal Air Force Regiment stop on a road while conducting a combat mission near Kandahar Airfield, Afghanistan

RIGHT: B Flight, 27 Squadron, Royal Air Force Regiment take a break whilst on a combat misson near Kandahar Airfield, Afghanistan

THE EUROFIGHTER TYPHOON

Developed by a consortium comprising Britain, France, Germany, Italy and Spain, the Eurofighter Typhoon was originally envisaged as a Mach 2 (at altitude) air superiority fighter, before it was realised that it also needed ground attack capabilities if it was to fully replace the Tornado with the RAF.

Recently, the aircraft has been upgraded to carry a number of different air-to-ground weapons, in particular the highly successful Brimstone missile. Its first combat missions came during the 2011 military intervention in Libya, where it displayed its new air-to-ground strike capabilities. It has gone to see action over both Iraq and Syria and currently provides QRA capability for the RAF as well as flying patrols over the Baltic.

MAIN IMAGE: A Royal Air Force Typhoon F2 fighter aircraft of 29 Squadron soars through the skies above its home base of RAF Coningsby

BELOW LEFT: Line drawing of Typhoon F2 fighter aircraft

OPP. PAGE T-B: Looking through the HUD; A Royal Air Force Typhoon pilot's helmet showing the Mounted Symbology System, which allows the pilot to see information from his instruments displayed on the visor of his helmet; Eurofighter AESA antenna CAPTOR-E with Wide Field of Regard Repositioner; A pilot's view from the cockpit of a Royal Air Force Typhoon multi role fighter jet

THE CUTS CONTINUE

With *'Austerity'* the political buzzword of the day, it was hardly surprising that David Cameron's Coalition government would choose to make deep defence cuts — an old favourite. For the Royal Air Force, The UK's Strategic Defence and Security Review in 2010 meant the cancellation of the Nimrod Maritime Patrol MR4, the early retirement — some might say premature — of the Harrier and a programme of closure of RAF bases.

WAR OVER LIBYA

In early 2011, a vicious civil war broke out in Libya as a variety of political and religious elements fought to bring down the local dictator, Colonel Muammar Gaddafi.

Operation Deference saw the RAF evacuating British civilians from Libya in mid-February 2011, a task shared with the Royal Navy. What began with orderly flights out of Benghazi with Hercules transports and Chinook helicopters ended with the last, desperate snatching up of civilians from remote desert airstrips. Over 8,000 British nationals and 1,000 others were successfully rescued.

RAF Typhoons and Tornados then went in action over Libya as part of Operation Ellamy, to create a *'No Fly Zone'* and to protect Libyan civilians. On the night of 19 March, RAF Tornados made their first attack with precision Storm Shadow munitions that were specifically designed to be used against hardened installations and weapons storage facilities. The Tornados flew out of RAF Marham in England and were refuelled four times en route during the course of their 3000 mile round trip mission by Tristar and VC10 tankers. It was the longest combat mission ever flown from the UK, and the Tornados scored eight direct hits from eight weapons fired. To provide essential intelligence and reconnaissance, the Tornados were supported by aircraft

including the Sentinel R1, E3D Sentry and Nimrod R1.

Ten Typhoons operating from an Italian air base were in action by 20 March. By 23 March the RAF announced that the Libyan Air Force *'no longer exists as a fighting force'* and Tornados now loaded up with Paveway IV and Brimstone munitions and prowled in search of any Libyan armour threatening civilians. On 12 April, Typhoons were used for ground attacks for the first time, expending Paveway II munitions to destroy Libyan tanks, and in the months that followed also went after rocket launchers and artillery. Operation Ellamy officially ended on 31 October 2011, by which time British forces were credited with damaging or destroying 870 enemy targets.

OPERATION SHADER

After the United States officially withdrew its troops from Iraq in December 2011, things very quickly fell apart into age-old religious conflict. Majority Shiites took the opportunity to use their muscle to oppress minority Sunnis, who had once ruled the country under Saddam. Fundamentalist Sunnis then got together with high ranking Sunni former military figures and together they created a new Jihadi force — ISIS — that staggered the world with its sheer brutality and savagery as it swept aside the Iraqi Army and seized control of major cities including Mosul.

In neighbouring Syria, the minority Shiites were in power under Bashar Assad. The majority Sunnis then rose up and initiated a civil war, during which ISIS elements seized large parts of the country and declared a caliphate with the city of Raqqa as their main base.

RAF operations in Iraq began as humanitarian efforts to help refugees displaced by ISIS in August 2014 with airdrops by C-130s on Mount Sinjar, where the minority Yazidi people had fled to escape ISIS's campaign

OPP. PAGE LEFT: Royal Air Force personnel from RAF Marham prepare a Tornado GR4 aircraft ahead of operations in support of UN Resolution 1973 to enforce the no-fly zone over Libya

OPP. PAGE RIGHT: A Tornado GR4 aircraft is pictured being prepared for a sortie during Operation Ellamy

BELOW: RAF C-17 at RAF Brize Norton is refueled before delivering humanitarian aid to Cyprus, for forwarding to Northern Iraq in support of Operation Shader

of genocide. Tornado GR4s were assigned to assist but strictly in a reconnaissance role. Drones followed.

Operation Shader officially began on 26 September 2014 after requests for help from the Iraqi government. At the end of September 2014, Parliament gave permission for the RAF to begin attacks on ISIS targets in Iraq. Defence Secretary Michael Fallon stated that the primary aim would be to stop the slaughter of civilians.

Initially, British attacks were carried out by Tornado GR4s. The first RAF Reaper drone attack came on 10 November 2014. Ten months later, the Reapers had flown over 1300 missions and launched some 300 attacks on ISIS targets. While attacks on Syria were not permitted by Parliament

MAIN IMAGE: RAF Tornado GR4 takes fuel from a Voyager tanker aircraft during an armed reconnaissance mission in support of Operation Shader

at this time, RAF pilots took part in strikes unofficially while embedded with USAF and the Canadian Air Force, and RAF aircraft and Reaper drones flew reconnaissance missions over Syria.

Throughout 2015, what ISIS was doing to civilians in Iraq and Syria became better known to the outside world. They were conducting mass executions of prisoners and beheading (on video) western kidnapping victims. Worse still, they were stoning or burning alive women on the slightest provocation, mounting children's heads on poles in playgrounds and holding grand *'Sex Slave Auctions'* where babies and toddlers fetched the highest prices. In June 2015, thirty British holidaymakers were murdered by an ISIS gunman on the beaches of Tunisia as ISIS sought to export its terror. Paris was attacked by ISIS in November. Things could not remain as they were. On 2 December 2015, Parliament finally gave permission for offensive operations against Syria. Within hours, four RAF Tornados from Cyprus bombed Omar oilfield in Eastern Syria — a target of considerable financial importance to ISIS.

By June 2016, RAF Tornados and Typhoons (along with drones) had conducted

around 900 airstrikes and killed an estimated 1,000 ISIS Jihadis across Syria and Iraq. By Christmas, it was said that the RAF was involved in its most intensive operations in a single theatre in 25 years. By April 2017, The RAF had flown more than 3,000 missions and launched over 1,200 airstrikes across Iraq and Syria, killing over 3,000 ISIS terrorists. A new determination had prevailed since 2017, as U.S. President Trump replaced Obama and set the Coalition ranged against ISIS on a much more aggressive footing. As of December 2017, ISIS is estimated to control no territory in Iraq, and just 5% of Syrian territory. In late January 2018, Fox News estimated that only 1,000 ISIS members remained. ISIS leaders have fled Syria, escaping to Afghanistan and parts of Africa, from where they hope to create a new caliphate. It would be premature to say the war is won.

MORE CHANGES

The Strategic Defence and Security Review 2015 was published on 23 November 2015 to outline the Britain's defence strategy up to 2025. It was of course shaped by the lessons being learned by Operation Shader. In it, the RAF were given permission to purchase nine P-8 Poseidon maritime patrol aircraft to fill the gap left by the 2010 cancellation of the Nimrod MRA4 and to increase total personnel levels by 300. The number of frontline Typhoon squadrons would be increased to seven by 2025, and aircraft upgraded so that they could serve until 2040. They would eventually be replaced by the Lockheed Martin F-35 Lightning, of which the government committed to initially ordering 138. The Tornado would cease service by 2019. By 2025, fourteen Voyager air-to-air refuelling aircraft will be in service with the RAF. Drone numbers would double, with the old Reapers giving way to more modern Protector drones.

As the Royal Air Force enters its second century, it is simply undeniable that it can look back on one hundred years of quite exceptional achievements and public service. Against the background of poor political judgement, Treasury parsimony and even ill-will, it has been called upon to complete the most difficult — sometimes impossible-seeming — tasks, and achieved success again and again against all odds. As and when times have required, it has been charged with protecting the nation, waging a world war, acting as a deterrent, extending British influence to remote parts of the world, combating guerrilla insurgencies and bringing emergency relief to stricken communities. It has done all these things, and done them supremely well, despite being manifestly limited in its resources. Its successes, conducted with skill, bravery and quiet professionalism, have won it the hearts of a nation — and made it the envy of many other air forces worldwide.

Today, the future of the RAF has been mapped out by recent reviews. The Tornado will soon give way to the Typhoon, which will itself be phased out by 2040 in favour of the Lockheed Martin F-35 Lightning II stealth multirole fighter. Some Hercules transports will be replaced by the Airbus A400M Atlas, while other Hercules will be kept on and upgraded to extend their service lives until 2035. The tanker fleet will come to rely on Airbus A330 Multi Role Tanker Transports. The retirement of the Ratheon Sentinel R1, which played such an important surveillance role in Afghanistan, has been delayed. The cancellation of the Nimrod MRA.4 in 2010 has led to a potentially dangerous gap in Britain's maritime patrol capability, but the gap is intended to be filled by the purchase of nine Boeing P-8A Poseidon aircraft. These would be introduced between 2018 and 2025, with armaments including torpedoes and Harpoon anti-ship missiles. Both Puma and Chinook helicopters are being upgraded to extend their service life. Three Boeing RC-135 Rivet Joint signals intelligence aircraft will remain in service for the foreseeable future. Reaper drones will be replaced by a newer Protector/Predator II model armed with Brimstones. This would be complimented by new Future Combat Air System (FCAS) drones and solar-powered Zephyrs, capable of spying on enemy nations from the edge of space.

This configuration could, however, be subject to change at any moment, as a government decides. This could be due to the recognition of new threats or priorities, or merely financial considerations. Ongoing Reviews are certain to shape the future of the RAF, as is raw political ideology. A Labour government might have very different priorities to a Conservative government. A greater consideration of British jobs or the awkward international legal tangles that come with subsidies could see a shift away from favouring American projects to supporting ones in which Britain holds a greater stake. Brexit may end up discouraging British involvement in European aviation in favour of a more global approach.

The RAF of the near future is being designed to fit well into an ongoing role with NATO. It is also shaped by known threats, some of which are very familiar indeed. Belligerent Russian adventurism from the Pole to the Ukraine has marked a return to some old Cold War thinking. Typhoon QRAs are now intercepting Putin's Bears, just as Lightnings and Phantoms once did. Islamic insurgencies stretching from Afghanistan to Iraq and Syria continue to boil — and the names of the towns and cities gripped by religious turmoil would have been all too familiar to the RAF airmen of the 1920s. Furthermore the increasing tensions between Sunni and Shiite nations — coupled with the desire for both sides to obtain nuclear weapons — could indicate a much larger conflagration on the horizon. The terrorist group ISIS now has a presence in 33 nations, meaning that the next call on the RAF might be in Africa. And then there are the impossible to predict conflicts. Whoever foresaw that the RAF would need to go to war with Argentina in 1982?

The RAF has benefitted a little from government favour in recent years, not least because its striking power provides a viable alternative to the dreaded *'boots on the ground'* — a strategy which at present is not just deeply unpopular with public opinion but also ruinously expensive in a world still mired in recession and in love with *'Austerity'* politics. Shades of the 1920s…

The ghost of Sandys is to be found here too. His review was premature but not wrong. Missiles are now at the sharp end of the nuclear deterrent. The debate has moved on now to how missiles can shoot down other missiles, rather than whether V-Bombers could survive SAMs at altitude. Bombers are now beasts of the battlefield rather than the ultimate death weapons of nations. There is considerable talk abroad that the F-35 may be the last RAF manned fighter. Tacticians and weaponeers see a future where fighter aces and *'Bomber Boys'* sit in secure rooms thousands of miles from the theatre of conflict and fly unmanned drones into battle via computers. Hackers will become the new anti-aircraft gunners.

This is all possible. It has a weary element of inevitability, given current demonstrations of Western government will. The gallantry and elan of generations of RAF pilots and crew may eventually be dissolved into a blizzard of electronic blips and squawks. The cavalry are gone from the battlefield and the RAF may follow them into obsolescence. It is equally possible, given the government's love of the word *'Joint'*, that the RAF along with the Royal Navy and Army will eventually merge into one indistinguishable (and no doubt cost-efficient) *'Joint Armed Force'*.

The only sure thing is, that as long as the RAF survives in a recognisable form, it will still continue to enjoy the respect, love and gratitude of the nation, to inspire legends, to represent that unique *'Air Spirit'* envisaged by Trenchard and to go out and do the impossible when called upon.

THE FUTURE OF THE ROYAL AIR FORCE